NAMING-DAY IN EDEN

THE MACMILLAN COMPANY
NEW YORK · CHICAGO
DALLAS · ATLANTA · SAN FRANCISCO
LONDON · MANILA

IN CANADA
BRETT-MACMILLAN LTD.
GALT, ONTARIO

NAMING-DAY
IN EDEN

The Creation
and Recreation of Language

By NOAH JONATHAN JACOBS

THE MACMILLAN COMPANY
New York   1958

Contents

Language Abbreviations Used in the Text

Algon., Algonquian
Amh., Amharic
Arab., Arabic
Aram., Aramaic
Chin., Chinese
Croat., Croatian
Dan., Danish
Dut., Dutch
Est., Estonian
Finn., Finnish
Fr., French
Gael., Gaelic
Ger., German
Goth., Gothic
Gr., Greek
Heb., Hebrew
Hung., Hungarian
It., Italian

Jap., Japanese
Lat., Latin
ME, Middle English
MHG, Middle High German
Nor., Norwegian
OE, Old English
OF, Old French
OHG, Old High German
Pol., Polish
Port., Portuguese
Rum., Rumanian
Russ., Russian
Serb., Serbian
Sp., Spanish
Swed., Swedish
Syr., Syrian
Swah., Swahili
Turk., Turkish

Introduction

Philosophic minds have always speculated on the nature of human speech. Countless learned works have been written dealing with the structure and classification of languages, their connections and points of divergence, their morphology and changing phonetic systems. These volumes often appear on poor paper with narrow margins and, what is worse, in German. They therefore cannot be recommended for continuous inspection by readers with weak eyes or wandering minds. Recent writers, guided by a positivistic bias, have attempted to disinfect language of its unpredictable elements and bring it close to logic and mathematics. We may secretly admire their erudition, but the jargon of their joyless tomes is so alarming that only intrepid souls imbued with a reckless love of the subject would venture beyond the opening lines. Yet no study is more rewarding or fascinating. Language touches on all subjects and overflows into every discipline. It exerts a direct and visible influence on our daily lives. The study of foreign tongues, the revival of ancient languages, the problems of translation, the adoption of a world language, the ethics of advertising, the ravages of propaganda and, above all, the vexing questions of correct speech—these are the subjects which fill the air with interminable quibbling, often breeding bad blood among the disputants. The great issues which perplex mankind, as well as its petty quarrels, revolve around words. The fate of many a man has been decided by a preposition or a conjunction. The controversies which convulsed the early Church, involving heresies which placed the very substance of Christian doctrine in jeopardy, were bound up with the deeper meaning of such simple words as *essence, sin, nature, person* and *begotten.* The tumult of these controversies has died down, but the force of the words used is still in the air around us and threatens from time to time to throw us into confusion.

This book deals with the age-old struggle of man with language. It emphasizes, from more familiar and comprehensive points of view, the place that language occupies in the various philosophical systems, its relation to rhetoric and its affiliations with religion, however eccentric that may appear to the modern temper. It begins with the story of Adam while he was still apricating amid the fragrant shrubs of Eden, eating fruit and nuts and chasing butterflies. It then relates the somber story of the Fall and its ensuing penalties, how Adam was stung by the serpent and betrayed by his Spare Rib, and how, finally, having forfeited his immortality, he chose to explore the mystery of his fallen nature in exile. Adam might have lived on in Eden in unbroken innocence had he not been hoodwinked by Eve and the serpent. But he stretched out his hand for the forbidden fruit, and we have reaped the disastrous consequences of his transgression. When he fell, prospectively considered, we all fell. Every man is related to Adam and relives the Fall daily. Adam, therefore, has more than local significance. He occupies the foremost place in the history of his race. More than any other man he has left on posterity the vivid marks of his personality and character. The autobiographical particulars of his rise and fall are the universal theme of literature and theology.

Of all the memorials of his genius none is more amazing than the gift of speech which he has bequeathed to us. We are in the dark concerning the nature of this miracle wrought by man's spirit. The origin and embryology of human speech are wrapped in mystery. All we know is that the first feeble sounds which broke forth from Adam have come down to us from ear to ear, the open gateway to the soul, and that the fatal sequence of that inexhaustible voice reverberating down the ages is the bond of solidarity which unites us in one continuous humanity. Adam's pioneering work in this field, his naming of the animals, has earned him a permanent niche in the science of linguistic investigation. In the symbolism of that mighty myth, as recorded in the second chapter of Genesis, we catch a glimpse of the grandeur of his creation and its significance in human history. The description of first man's linguistic activity as described in these two short verses is the slender foundation on which this volume is erected:

> And out of the ground the Lord God formed every beast of the field and every fowl of the air, and brought them unto Adam to see what he would call them: and whatsoever Adam called every living creature, that was the name thereof. And Adam gave names to all cattle, and to the fowl of the air, and to every beast of the field; but for man there was not found an help meet for him.
>
> Genesis 2:19–20

 I *Man's Finest Hour*

Adam was barely one hour old on that fateful fall morning in the springtime of the world (October 4, 4004 B.C., as computed by that exact theologian Bishop Butler) when the Lord assembled the inhabitants of the newly formed earth and paraded them before Adam to see what he would call them. Adam grasped the situation at a glance. He surveyed the line-up before him and, his moist eye, unencumbered by glass or monocle and in a fine frenzy rolling, gave to each of the marchers, whom he now beheld for the first time, a local habitation and a name. In the very infancy of the world man was able to create a symbolic net to capture the fleeting objects before him and make them the object of his intellectual knowledge. With his invisible breath he devised unheard-of names, substantial enough to be freighted with deep thoughts and mobile enough to waft their precious cargo down the ages. God had created the earth, and Adam festooned it with a web of words. With this second creation man gave the world its first constitution. In language he found a foothold and a lever to move the solid world. The verbal execution of this conception deserves the highest praise because it was the greatest single achievement of the human mind and bears the indispensable marks of genius. What man since the Fall, what Solomon

1

among the ancients or Leibniz among the moderns, nay, what logical positivist could undertake such a prodigious task? The prediluvian exploit of the patriarch Noah who, with the help of his wife and wicked sons, rounded up the animals and persuaded them to enter the Ark was a menial chore compared to primal man's linguistic feat. Adam himself stood aghast at the phantom world he had unchained. He could not believe his own ears. *Homo nascitur poeta*, Adam was born a poet. No other animal could have created such an elaborate linguistic edifice, because no animal has the necessary intellectual vigor to represent the world in symbolic forms, unless it were, as the Scotch philosopher Monboddo suggested, that patient architect the beaver.

Armed with this verbal mechanism, man was able to break through every barrier which imprisoned his spirit to assume a commanding position of supremacy. On a bridge of words formed by his lips he crossed the narrow isthmus which separated him from the animals. Halfway across the *pons asinorum*, with one foot in eternity, he looked before him into History (not without misgivings) and behind him on the natural life of Instinct (not without envy, for how could he forget his past?) and, drawing a deep breath, named the cowering beasts as they marked time before him. With these names man drew a line (later ignored by the behaviorists) between the lower animals and himself and thus established his sovereignty over an alien world. This was man's finest hour. He had dissolved the bonds of his origin and had leaped headlong to his new position of freedom, while the incorrigible beasts, loath to break their chains with the past, crept back to their lairs on all fours. They were too absorbed in the satisfaction of their feverish appetites to risk a rupture with their instincts, too steeped in primitive felicity to follow the beckoning ideal. Had they evinced the slightest inclination for that celestial metamorphosis, God would have lent them a Hand. But they stood aside and cried "Nay." They deserved to be left behind.

Numerous instances of animal sagacity have been recorded by psychologists who have made extensive phonetic researches into the sounds with which the animal world regales us. With their customary effrontery these investigators have looked down the throats of animals in an effort to decipher their dark sayings (in the case of the lion from outside the cage) and have made careful notes on the timbre, tempo and motifs of their vocalizations. Extraordinary mental feats have been revealed by these field auditions. On one occasion a horse was observed working out square roots and a dog was overheard dictating his last will and testament to his spouse as he wiped a tear from his eye. A religious instinct has been detected in the praying mantis (Gr. *mántis*, prophet), a grasshopper that folds its forelegs in an attitude of prayer, and in the elephant, who turns to the east at sundown as it lifts its trunk in worship. It is reported that monkeys, when not involved in arboreal distractions, can speak our language but refrain from doing so lest they be mistaken for men. The experts have also compiled librettos of the woodland concerts of the modulated rhythms of the warbler, the syncopations of the cuckoo and the starling's plagiarisms. The most impressive examples, however, are the recorded bits of human speech of the gifted ibis (venerated by the Egyptians as the inventor of the clyster) and the small talk of the pewit, which is known as the exegete among the birds, for it feeds on delicacies hidden under rocks and excels in interpreting danger signals to its companions.

These vernal researches, though elaborately conducted, are not well authenticated. They exaggerate the mental processes of animals and attribute to them powers they do not possess. The rhinoceros, for example, is extremely dull and short-tempered. Silly hens have been persuaded to sit on addled eggs for days on end. The magpies, lapwings and jackdaws (known in German as *Litauer*, Lithuanians, because of their raucous *k*'s and *r*'s) say harsh things to one another in torrents of excessively bad language. Some birds, as the stork and the woodpecker, are incapable of producing vocal sounds, and some animals, notably the white cat (if it has blue eyes), are stone deaf. It is true that few animals are wholly silent. From the very outset, even before man appeared, each had its own mode of expression when in a talking mood—the asses brayed, the moles rumbled, the doves moaned, the plovers whistled, the gnats hummed, the turtles wept, the monogamous rhinoceros yawned and the lovely elephant blew his trumpet. The fishes too uttered amorous phrases, too delicate for our coarse ears to perceive. But it was an absurd concert wasted on the desert air, for no one really listened. However extraordinary the vocal efforts of animals, they are debarred from human articulation. Speech does not depend on physical endowment but on the wit to connect sound with purpose. The animals are not phonetically defective but semantically blocked. Their speech is hence an unchanging dialect, incapable of variation or improvement, consisting of a limited repertory of vague interjections which are not intended to convey knowledge but merely to voice subjective fears. The duck's dialect, for example, is confined to a monosyllabic, exiguous quack, devoid of variety, wit or compass. The frog's inflections are as infantile and spasmodic today as in the days of Aristophanes. The parrots are generally regarded as having mastered our speech technique, but their speech is unoriginal and profane, and their diction is obscured by an excessive nasality which they have in common with the Puritans, originating in both species from a sanctimonious drawl intoned through cavernous hooked noses. It is true that the serpent's conversation with Eve was marked by careful diction and close reasoning and that Baalam's ass on one occasion indulged in repartee. But the serpent was soon deprived of his gift of speech for abusing his prerogative, and the ass never repeated his initial inspired performance. Man alone is articulate. When an ass speaks, it is a miracle.

It cannot be denied that Adam enjoyed unparalleled advantages in Eden. The Himalayan air of the Garden was favorable to his brooding genius and conducive to "learned leisure." In its solitude, undisturbed by visitors, servants or the clamorous exigencies of domestic life, he found ample material for the application of original principles. Yet Adam labored under incomparable difficulties. He was young in years, anonymous, unchastened by the miscellaneous lessons of experience and hence prone to errors of judgment. His life had struck root in a congenial soil, in the very umbilicus of the world, but his view was confined to the landscape of Eden. Although he was not compelled to submit his random cogitations to a human tribunal for approval, he had no traditional models to emulate, no reference works or maps to consult. There is no more impressive example in history of such an unnatural divorce between inborn talent and acquired experience. His untutored mind was an empty sheet, as Locke assures us, blank on both sides. His chief drawback, however, was neither immature judgment nor inherited weaknesses, but the absence of those powerful incentives to progress: money, alcohol and the fury of fashion.

Nevertheless, our indomitable First Ancestor pressed on with self-assurance. Here was a rank outsider, an orphan and a bachelor to boot, who stepped forward to the dizzy edge and took possession of the world. He accepted his uniqueness. Why could not his horizontal companions rise above themselves to an upright position and escort man to freedom? They could not take off on the wings of abstraction because they failed to understand the nature of language. Hence, they were left to sniff their way along a cul-de-sac while man set out on a limitless road to make his mark in the world.

5

II *The Companions Adam Left Behind*

Adam's bold step toward freedom introduced new features of violence into the world and seriously disturbed the balance between the plant and the animal kingdoms. His sudden departure must have been regarded by the others as a breach of loyalty on the part of a degenerate member who had lost his sound animal sense. They classified their poor relation as a zoological freak, a beast with brains, a man fallen from monkeyhood, and then they returned to their sensible round of duties. Naturally, they refused to follow him to the perilous frontier so far removed from corporeal being, except the dog, who followed his master's whistle with cynegetical fidelity. The dog is aware of his own worthlessness. Waggish, cynical, a slave to wretched odors, he is constantly sniffing about as if he had lost something irrecoverable. The unauthentic bark, which displaced the original wild howl, is the vocal expression of the dog's synechthrous attachment to man. The other animals, especially the cat, show superior judgment in avoiding man altogether, regarding it as a misfortune to be in his vicinity. Their interests are in conflict and differ on vital issues. Man looks upon animals as game to be hunted, reduced to servitude, roasted and eaten (sometimes alive, like the pensive oyster). Moreover, he ridicules them and deliberately wounds their self-respect. His hostility to cats and owls is well known. He has tormented the horse and made a nervous wreck of this aristocratic stable creature, as is evident from its hysterical laugh and the jerky movements of its head.

Man paid a high price for his superiority and in his heart he felt that he had perhaps gone too far in the wrong direction. He was in peril and he knew it. His feet pointed to the green roots of animal life and his head to the frail flower of human culture, an intolerable position in the long run. To go too far forward into a world of fiction and abstraction is to be cast adrift from the solid moorings in the senses; to go back is to lose access to the intelligible world of freedom and history. He was the center of two incompatible impulses equally imperious and with no discernible principle of reconciliation. His new position filled him with an anxiety common to dominant individuals, a fear of having his pretensions challenged and of tumbling from his eminence. This produced in him a congenital vacillation and involved him in a web of baffling problems he could neither solve nor avoid, doomed to tarry at the crossroads, a *parvus mundus* of opposites:

> How poor, how rich, how abject, how august,
> How complicate, how wonderful is man.
> An heir of glory, a frail child of dust,
> Helpless immortal, insect infinite,
> A worm or God. I tremble at myself.
> O what a miracle to man is man:
> Triumphantly distressed, what joy, what dread,
> Alternately transported and shamed.
>   —Young, *Night Thoughts*

This perpetual discord of man with himself moved Pascal to lay down for himself the following line of conduct in relation to his

7

fellow men: "It is dangerous to let man see too clearly how he is on a level with the animals without showing him his greatness . . . or to let him see too clearly his greatness without his meanness. If he boast, I abase him; if he abases himself, I exalt him . . . till he comprehends what an incredible monster he is."

Adam did not turn his back completely on the companions he left behind. He carried them along within him, especially the vulture and the ass. His human task was neither to renounce the ancestral brutes nor to identify himself with them, but to harness and subdue them to his larger ends. He would give his life in search for the truth, and find if he could the rational elements of reality. But this complicated, never ending process wearied his mind, and he was forced from time to time to return from his cerebral adventures, in accordance with Locke's wingless doctrine, to the sensuous impressions imbedded in his organism. After the highest flights of abstract thought the overtaxed mind seeks a resting place, like Noah's dove, on some material twig. Now and then, as if stirred by a redeeming wind, man seeks to terminate his loneliness, to forget his class consciousness, and to revert to the economy and vigor of animal life. Such a reunion with his dumb brethren is effected in two fundamentally different ways: either man descends to the level of the beast or he raises them to his level; either he regards man as a good ape gone wrong or he regards the ape as an unfallen man. The first is the method of naturalism, the second that of romanticism.

In the naturalistic view man's vaunted superiority is unjustified. The beasts appear dumb only to his dull perceptions. No beast can be so bestial and brutish as man, no animal so depraved, intemperate and contemptible. He devours more flesh than all the animals together. Man has been betrayed by his aberrant reason. Even his instinct for self-preservation has been lost. He eats foods which shorten his life, and often dies of ptomaine poisoning or excessive alcohol. It is true that some animals, like the goat and the caterpillar, do not possess fastidious palates and that the camel is careless in his diet, often mistaking white stones for lumps of salt. But, by and large, their errors are not fatal. A so-called lower animal would have sniffed the apple and rejected it. Adam ate the obnoxious fruit and did irreparable damage to his digestive tract. That a sound diet is the beginning of wisdom and the key to history was already noted by Feuerbach who attributed the superiority of the English to their diet of beef and urged the Irish to replace potatoes with beans, the food of revolution. In reality, however, England owed its superiority to its old maids, as a distinguished British biologist has pointed out. For good English beef, his argument runs, depends upon the industrious bumblebee which pollinates red clover eaten by cattle, and the number of bumblebees in turn is determined by the number of cats, since the mice rob the nests of the bumblebees, and mice are killed by cats. Hence, few cats mean many mice, few bumblebees, little clover and bad meat. Because old maids are fond of cats as pets, ergo England's power depends on the number of its old maids.

Some overzealous naturalists have not only succeeded in imitating animals but in actually *becoming* animals, as Nebuchadnezzar who ate grass with the oxen. This affliction, which is known as boanthropy, is not common nowadays, but traces of it can be detected in our salad-eating enthusiasts. Some tribes in South Africa resort to knocking out their teeth in order to look like the ox. The adoption of the name John Bull as the national symbol of England has been regarded by discerning psychologists as incriminating evidence of the presence of subconscious boanthropic tendencies in the inhabitants of that country.

It is linguistic usage, however, that offers the most disconcerting evidence to attest to our animal origins. A number of surnames (3 per cent in English) are derived from animals, as Hogg, Fox,

Crabbe, Beaver, Columbus (Lat. *columba*, dove), and so on, the stable alone having furnished a large variety (compare Chekhov's charming story "A Horsy Name"). Unlovely animal traits, real or fancied, give mournful proof of our lowly origin—disrespectful epithets, as *catty*, *asinine*, *bird-witted*, *capricious*, *fawning;* appellations, as *coxcomb*, *roadhog*, *skunk;* and from the realm of bird life, *guttersnipe*, *stool-pigeon*, *jailbird* and *jinx*. *Camel* is in Turkish an epithet for an awkward person, in German for a blockhead and in French for a blighter, rotter or trollop; *owl* in English connotes solemn wisdom, in French a moper (*hibou*), in Arabic a Calamity Jane (*boomeh*), in Spanish an owlish woman (*lechuza*) and in German a queer duck (*ein sonderbarer Kauz*) or a gay dog (*ein lustiger Kauz*). In French *maquereau* (mackerel) is a pimp, *poule* (hen) a loose woman, and *une mouche du coche* (a fly on the coach-wheel) a busybody. A long catalogue of unflattering epithets derived from the animal world to describe the crotchets and caprices of men is to be found in the bestiary lore of every language, usually based on erroneous conceptions of animal behavior. The furtive beast is seen lurking in a disquieting number of our fellow men. Gracian observed that at twenty man is a peacock, at thirty a lion, at forty a camel, at fifty a serpent, at sixty a dog, at seventy an ape and at eighty nothing at all. Tischbein, a keen observer of men, is said to have remarked to a stranger in Naples: "Excuse me, I mistook you at first for an ass, but I see now that you are really an ox." These insights extend as well to the highest intellectual circles. Swinburne called Arnold "the most unending ass in Christendom," and Carlyle described Emerson as "a gap-toothed and hoary ape," protesting he was using language of the strictest reserve.

Romanticism seeks unity in nature by a return to the sensible world, our root and anchor. Impelled by an all-embracing love, man finds his place among the beasts, albeit in a privileged position. His attitude to the animals is one of sympathy and reverence rather than one of superiority. In primitive man this union is effected by an alliance with certain animals (totemism) which embody dead souls, or by the sacrifice of consecrated animals in an effort to appease them (animal cults). The doctrine of signatures refers to the acquisition of an animal nature by mimetic masked dances imitating beasts or by eating a certain part of an animal in order to acquire its characteristics; for example, eating an animal tongue imparts eloquence, lion's meat courage, and so on. The later Romantic theory assumed that the animal world was not involved in the Fall and has hence preserved its innocence in an uncorrupted state. Instead of degrading man, as in the boanthropy of the naturalist, Romantics elevate the beasts with their theriophilism. The unaffected, lowly ass was singled out for adulation (onolatry), chiefly as a dramatic way of humbling man's pride in decorum and reason (compare Wordsworth's *Peter Bell* and Hugo's *Legend of an Ass*). Proper names were selected from the milder aspects of animal life: Lamb bore a name which was appropriate to his meek nature and Cowper's name reminded Hazlitt of the dove's low cooing, awakening a stealthy tenderness in him. Much religious instruction has been gained from the unedifying traits of animals, from the salaciousness of the cock, the vindictiveness of the rat, the pride of the peacock, the greed of the vulture, the affected humility of the cat and the extortionist practices of the caterpillar. In Christianity the pelican became the symbol of the Redeemer because it feeds its young with its own blood, and the phoenix, rising from its ashes, the symbol of the Resurrection. The very name of the Saviour was seen in the famous acrostic of the initial letters of five Greek words which form the word for fish, *ichthus*. In religion man's dignity is not impaired by a comparison with animals. David with true humility called himself a worm, a dead dog and a flea; and Jerome referred to himself as a louse (*ego pulex*). But when Vanini in 1616 suggested that man *was* a quadruped, he was promptly burned as a heretic. For man shares with the animals only his body, as Descartes taught, but not his soul. It remained for our age to *identify* man with the animal and to seek the clue to his essence in the behavior of rats in mazes or in the tropisms of plant lice.

III *Adam Names the Animals*

How did it dawn on first man to use his invisible breath to express the ideas stirring within him? Spirit alone is formless and empty; language alone seduces us from the truth with its syntax and euphony. Which of the two mandates did Adam follow? The problem was how to introduce opaque language into spirit without obscuring it. How did the sounds Adam uttered capture the essence of the animals that passed before him in review? Was the conjunction of the airy concept and the palpable intuition fortuitous? Were the animal names invented for the occasion or were they stored up in some divine greenhouse waiting to be selected by Adam's brooding mind? Did the bewildered beasts fall noiselessly into place when their master's voice fell upon them and slip into their names as if into preexisting garments? And if Adam created these garments a priori, on what principles were the patterns cut? Would another man differently disposed have created other designs? Did man aim his arrowy words at the target's center or was his bow struck at a venture? And if shot from his primal brain in happy ignorance, how did those random verbal darts find their fleshy marks to brand them forever? But our Great Progenitor proceeded confidently and with an air of strong assurance. He himself seems to have set high store on his performance. After he had reviewed the Parade, we see him pacing to and fro, soliloquizing on the import of his linguistic feat, which he straightway made the subject of a panegyric:

> I named them as they passed, and understood
> Their nature; with such knowledge God endued
> My sudden apprehension. . . .
>
> *Paradise Lost,*
> BOOK VIII, ll. 352–354

What *was* the nature of that "sudden apprehension"? Of the infinity of natural sounds ringing in his ears, which did Adam choose to render the essence of the tabanid horsefly, the piebald magpie, the aciculated hedgehog, the wanton lapwing, and all the animals which in that brief review frolicked before him on the green? Was the name he gave the elephant, for example, a faithful reproduction of its roaring (the bow-wow theory) or of some mystic harmony between it and the sound that its vast trunk emitted when struck (the ding-dong theory)? Was the name a rhythmic chant designed to raise its flagging spirit as man goaded it on to do his work (the yo-heave-ho theory) or a vocal reflex signifying his displeasure (the pooh-pooh theory)? It may be that Adam's tongue unwittingly reproduced some typical elephantine gesture, an oral replica of the beast's lithe proboscis, the texture of its wrinkled bulk or the swish of its flapping tail (the ta-ta or the wig-wag theory). Or, to take a more modest example, how did Adam name the bat? Which characteristic impressed him at the moment of naming? Did its blindness move him to call it *murciélago* (Sp.), its baldness *chauve-souris* (Fr.), its shyness *pipistrello* (It.), its leathery skin *Laderlapp* (Dan.) or *böregér* (Hung. from *bör*, leather; *egér*, mouse), its preference for the night *nukteris* (Gr.), its resemblance to the mouse *Fledermaus* (Ger.) or *letutsaya mysh* (Rus.), the sound of its flapping wings *watwat* (Arab.), its winglike hands *chiroptera* (Lat. from

14

Gr. *chir*, hand, plus *pteron*, wing), its resemblance to a lily (!)
liliac (Rum.), its reputed love of bacon *bat* (OE *backe*, bacon)?
The Chinese have conferred a number of laudatory names on this
mouselike mammal, such as *embracing wings, heavenly rat, fairy
rat, night swallow*, and use it as a symbol of happiness and long
life because its name *fu* in Chinese happens to be a homonym
which means both *bat* and *prosperity*.

The truth of the matter seems to be that in the short time at his
disposal, roughly about thirty minutes, Adam was obliged to employ a number of linguistic devices. The beasts had first to be
divided into hoofed and clawed, and the former subdivided into
cloven and noncloven hoofed. The question of gender then
obtruded itself, and this Adam solved by composition (*she-
elephant, nanny goat*), by addition of a suffix (*lioness, tigress*),
by inverse deduction, deriving the male from the female
(*goose-gander, duck-drake, cat-tomcat*); and by suppletion,
that is, by supplying new forms (*ram-ewe, boar-sow, dog-bitch*).
Where the mode of propagation escaped detection because of its
rapidity or obscurity, making a responsible decision impossible
(as in the case of the rabbit, the turtle and the elephant), Adam
disregarded the distinction of sex. The other criteria at his disposal were:

a) place of origin: the *great Dane*, the *Pekingese, Scotty,
spaniel* (Spain) and the *tarantula* (Lat. Tarentum, now Taranto
in Sicily);

b) size: the *horsefly*, the *bumblebee*, the *bug* (akin to *big*?),
and the *chameleon* (Gr. *khamaí*, dwarf, plus *léon*, lion);

c) means of sustenance: the *linnet* which feeds on the seeds
of flax and hemp (Lat. *linum*, flax), the *anteater* and the *fish
crow;*

d) characteristic sounds emitted: the *bullfrog*, whose croak
resembles a bull's roar; the *catbird*, whose call is like the mewing

of a cat; and the *partridge* (Gr. *pérdix*, applied to one who expels wind), from the sound it makes when rising;

e) shape: the *ringworm*, the *spoonbill duck*, the *crossbill* and the *fiddler crab*, which holds its large claw as a fiddler his bow;

f) method of locomotion: the *grasshopper*, *adelopodes* (animals whose feet are hidden), *reptiles* (Lat. *repere*, to creep), *dromedary* (Gr. *dromas*, running—about nine miles an hour), *bustard* (OF *bistarde*, from Lat. *avis tarda*, slow-walking bird), *duck* (from *ducking*) and *dove* (from *diving*);

g) color: the *redbreast*, the *hare* (related to *hazy*, *gray*), the *oppossum* (Algon. *apasum*, white beast), the *penguin* (Welsh *pen*, head, plus *gwyn*, white), the *pygarg*, a kind of antelope with white hindquarters (Gr. *pugé*, rump, plus *argós*, white), *albatross* (corruption from Lat. *albus*, white, plus Port. *alcatras*, cormorant) and *beaver* (OE *beofor*, brown);

h) odor exuded: the *muskrat* (from its musky smell), the *pismire*, from the urinous smell of an anthill (ME *pissemyre*, from *piss*, plus *mire*, ant), and the Ger. *Stinktier*, skunk;

i) facial expression: the *dodo* (Port. *doudo*, stupid);

j) mode of scratching: *racoon* (Algon. *arathcone*, he scratches with his hands);

k) mode of excretion: the *butterfly*, whose excrement resembles butter, and the *shitepoke heron*, because of the way it empties its bowels when frightened by a shot.

When confronted with two or more criteria, demanding a split decision, Adam adopted more than one name: *turkey* (Turkey) and Fr. *coq d'Inde* (India); *pewit*, from its cry, or *lapwing*, from its motion (OE *hleápan*, to leap, plus *winc*, to totter); the name of the *owl*, which he at first mistook for a feathered cat, he derived from its doleful hooting (Eng. owl, (h)owl; Lat. *ulula*, Swah. *babewatoto*) and also from its glaring eyes (Gr. *glauks* from *glaúkos*, blue, gray, hence glaring); Finn. *pöllö*, owl = staring eyes, *pöllöpää*, to gape; the *lynx* received its name from its light color or from its sharp eyes. An additional factor which complicated Adam's task was the relative distance between the animals and himself. This determined the length of the vowels in the name because the tongue, in accordance with a theory now associated with the name of Piaget but which goes back to Aulus Gellius and Nigidius Figulus, instinctively imitates the space relation of the namer's body to the object, so that the vowels made with the shortened tongue are attached to the animals close by, as the *hen*, the *lamb* or the *squirrel*, and those made with the protruding tongue are extended to those farther removed, as the *mole*, the *cow* and the *owl*.

Adam did not permit himself to be diverted by deceptive sounds or arbitrary combinations at the expense of good sense as did poets of a later age. He did not exploit "apt alliteration's artful aid" to suggest the clatter of hoofbeats (Virgil), hissing serpents (Racine) or the progress of rats (Browning's "The Pied Piper"). Sound alone, which beguiles the ear without engaging the mind, is an unreliable vehicle for thought. The commonplace must not be made alluring by tawdry adornment; the mule's head need not be hung with tinkling bells. Adam called the horse a horse and not Pegasus, the lion a lion and not the father of roaring, the camel a camel and not the ship of the desert. His aim was not to copy reality in every detail in the manner of the "material imitation" of the pre-Platonic philosophers who regarded language as a passive stamp of reality, every sound having an innate quality which makes it suitable to represent certain ideas; he followed Plato's theory of "ideal imitation" where a word expresses the inner essence of a thing, the meaning behind the ever changing object. This view is rejected by those who hold to the "convention theory" according to which words acquire meaning not from their sounds but by common agreement. A word merely provides an appropriate mode of conveying our thoughts, and its meaning is defined by custom and mutual agreement. The sound of a word tells us as little about its meaning as a key about the contents of a room or a seashell about the marine life that haunts the deep. Adam could have given different names to the same creature (Eng. *ewe*, Arab. *najat*) or the same name (Eng. *ewe*, Hung. *juh*); or two different animals could have received the same name (Eng. *dog*, Heb. *dag*, fish). This is the ever recurrent argument advanced against the theory of "ideal imitation" since the days of the Sophists when Democritus refuted Heraclitus: there is no natural connection between a word and the thing it designates. But Adam's names could not have been submitted to anyone for agreement by the very nature of the case. They rang true of their own accord because his speech was a reflection of his reason, his *oratio* flowed from his *ratio*. That is, his basic agreement did not come from the arbitrary corroboration of mortal men but from God who inspired him with the breath of life and who vouched for his speech, as we shall see in the next chapter.

IV *The Joust with the Devil*

A rabbinic legend which has come down to us represents the naming scene in the Garden as a verbal contest or spelling bee among Adam, the angels and the Devil. The angels, of course, were the first to be eliminated, for angels are notoriously poor linguists. They are too conceited (that is, conceptual), and since they speak to God face to face, their diaphanous words are defecated of all opaqueness. Their sensuous functions have been extinguished so that they have no idea of sensible images, metaphor, tones or gestures. They have no need in their noumenal sphere of these seductive and puzzling artifices. Their penchant for unashamed abstraction is the deepest strain in their make-up. The thick facts in the redundant realm of feeling are totally foreign to the angelic mood. Eliminated in the very first round, the angels retired behind the Lord to watch the principals from the background. On the other side, infant History, still unoccupied, was wistfully awaiting the incubation of the second creation. We now see Adam emerging from the wings of the green stage, skipping his way amid the fragrant foliage. The Devil then entered from the north on horseback, as is his custom. Adam, though chaste and vigorous, was no match for the Devil, whose impetuous mind, unburdened by moral scruples and sharpened in the struggle with virtue, was fit to rend into pieces the most recalcitrant material. He was even then an expert in language, a past master of polyptoton, epanados, opomnemonysis, anacoenosis and persiflage, and could quote Scripture by heart. He knew the hang of things in this hurly-burly world of illusion and deception. His aggressive mind hankered after concrete ideas in the world of flesh. He never lost sight of the innumerable portents of mortality in the stubborn world of sense, the material base that lies at the root of words—the eye in *daisy* (OE *daeges éage*, day's eye), the ass in *easel* (Dut. *ezel*, ass), the groove in *delirium* (Lat. *de* plus *lira*, furrow, that is, not in the groove), the buttocks in *recoil* (Lat. *re* plus *culus*, the posteriors) and the testicles in *orchid* (Gr. *órkhis*, testicle). The Devil, unlike the angels, was at home in the world of phenomena. He knew how to combine pure concepts with empirical intuitions, the sound with the inner form, which is the basic principle of linguistic creation. No wonder he was self-assured and confident of victory.

The Lord then passed before the contestants the ox, the camel and the ass, in the order named. A Midrashic footnote informs us that only *one* animal, namely, the ox, was presented, since the Hebrew text gives only the singular form: "And the Lord brought *it* to Adam to see what he would call *it*." This, however, could only mean that Adam was still unfamiliar with the plural number. The dual number was first devised by Noah, according to the available linguistic data, when he reviewed the animals two by two as they embarked. To Adam, however, the animals were presented one by one until the zoological parade was completed, with the exception of the pig and the cat, which were created later in Noah's Ark, the pig being formed from the elephant's trunk in order to dispose of the accumulated garbage and the cat being sneezed forth by the lion so as to rid the boat of rats. In any case, the Devil, heckled by the unfriendly spectators, became rattled and failed to give the proper names to the first three animals presented. Thereupon Adam, without hesitation, pronounced the right names and was hailed victor. How did he contrive to win the contest against such superior odds?

At this point a rabbinic tradition comes to our rescue with an amazing particular not generally known; namely, that this verbal duel had been previously "fixed" by the Lord, who deliberately revealed to Adam the proper answers by a mnemonic device concealed within the question; that is, the Divine Interlocutor framed the questions in such a manner that the first letter of the first word of the question was the same as the first letter of the name of the animal under consideration. The Devil had hoped for little sympathy but he was not prepared for this unscrupulous ruse. It turned his enthusiasm to bitterness. As soon as he detected the unethical stratagem, he retired to the shades vowing vengeance. His chagrin spurred him to undertake the most arduous tasks. After he had planned and executed the Fall, he was condemned to the confines of the netherworld. He managed to escape later by hiding behind the donkey when it was taken into the Ark before the Deluge. Since then the Devil has had his tail in everything. He has invented paper money, dabbled in chemistry and has learned to play all the instruments in the orchestra, although having a marked preference for the French horn. He is also credited with the authorship of the largest Bible in existence, the so-called Devil's Bible, which is preserved in the Royal Library of Stockholm. The Manichean heretics were impressed with these achievements, and concluded that he had created at least half of the world and that we are all made in his image. His cleverest ruse, however, has been to convince the moderns (except the Scots, who claim to possess his tomb at Kirkcaldy, the birthplace of Adam Smith) that he does *not* exist. If true, this would be a great blow to the theologians. The Devil himself, however, has recorded that he loves humanity more than man who has outdeviled him a hundredfold (compare Leonid Andreyev's *Satan's Diary* for a moving account of his torments at the hands of men).

Now, from this divine Intervention at the very dawn of human history we can gain a number of linguistic and pedagogical insights of prime importance. In the first place it is evident that Adam in naming the animals applied a priori principles not derived from his own meager experience. That is, the God-given rational principle, which is the *conditio sine qua non* of all knowledge, was already part of man's mind and operative in the spiritual activity of naming, else he would not have understood God's promptings. Abravanel of Portugal, the last of the Jewish Aristotelians at the time of Columbus, formulated this principle as follows: "God created language according to nature; and when He created man, He created in him the principles of language." This formulation is based on the phrase "and man became a living soul" (Genesis 2:7), which in the Aramaic translation, obviously influenced by the Stoics, is rendered "and the breath of life became in man a speaking spirit." Corroboration for this rational conviction has been found by exegetes in the verb *to see* in our text (Genesis 2:19), from which they deduce that the Lord was watching Adam during the contest, just as a teacher watches his pupil, *to see* whether the lesson had been learned well. From this we learn that God is the Author of language, that He imparted it to Adam when He prompted him to name the animals He presented to his gaze, and that man "caught on" because God had condescended to breathe the breath of life into the dust He had formed so that He could speak to man on common ground. This divine Whispering holds things together in the perceptual world and is the guarantee of the validity of human communication. Prayer precedes speech, and words have meaning only in relation to the Word. The collaboration between the human and the divine gives language its substance. Adam thus becomes the

Interpreter of the divine, which is the proper function of the prophet.

The Devil, with all his prodigious learning, could not withstand this sagacious division of labor. He knew the law, but Adam knew the Judge of whose protection he was assured: "And I have put my words in thy mouth, and I have covered thee in the shadow of mine hand, that I may plant the heavens and lay the foundations of the earth" (Isaiah 51:16). The animals could have been named by the Lord, but He relegated the task to Adam for pedagogical reasons, to summon him to use his reason, to make him responsible in a dialogic situation and to give him the opportunity for re-creation. Though God could have prompted Adam with the entire name of the animal in question, He preferred to give him only the first letter, a mere hint. For each man must appropriate the truth on his own as a free act of ethical choice. Repetition by rote deprives the student of the challenge to make decisions by increasing his dependence upon the teacher. A teacher's precepts should be deliberately vague, since the circumstances in life are too varied and intricate for the arbitrary application of specific rules. The function of the teacher is to present problems, not solutions; to give yeast, not bread. Truth does not fall into the student's mouth like a ripe apple. Thus did God convey His purposes to Adam in this first lesson. God was the coining master, but Adam had to learn the value of money through his own responsible labors.

We must now consider briefly some disquieting ethical implications of this divine Intervention which the Devil found so reprehensible. There is a touch of "splendid wickedness" worthy of Machiavelli in God's violating the rules of fair play by concealed promptings. This poses an awkward ethical problem. Fortunately, this moral paradox has been solved by Hegel's doctrine of "the cunning of reason" and Adam Smith's principle of "the invisible hand," both of which justify God's action in retrospect.

Naming-Day in Eden

Adam was the instrument, according to Hegel, of an ulterior rational design of the World Spirit. The two collaborators were not confronted with a moral issue but with a technical problem: how to outwit the Devil and advance the cause of historical development. What would we think of Adam if he had followed Feuerbach's humanitarian teachings and had dealt honorably with the Devil, relying on the latter's mercy and self-restraint? What appears to be benevolence is often folly, and what appears to be a vice may serve a superior end but dimly perceived. "Cunning reason" thus uses the private aims and personal motives of men as a lever of historical development. Similar to this doctrine is Adam Smith's principle of "the invisible hand," its economic counterpart. Private vices turn to public benefits. Self-love is not an opprobrious epithet. Prudently directed, it is "a splendid vice" which promotes progress and opulency though it is not part of the original intention. Led by an "invisible hand," self-interest becomes the mainspring of personal achievement and the guarantee of the general welfare.

Adam's first encounter with the Devil centered upon linguistic problems and throws much light on the study of languages. The first and highest aim of the student of language is to know the Author of language and to be on good terms with Him, to listen modestly to His whisperings (which are not in opposition to his own self-interest) and not to be diverted by an unconscious stream of imagery or by abstract altruistic principles. Then, though he may irritate the Devil, he will have no cause to fear him.

 V *Names to Conjure With*

In the joust with the Devil man and God united their efforts in a student-teacher relationship against a common enemy. They had not yet entered into a genuine personal relationship. This involved a ceremonious exchange of first names as customary in order to make informal dialogue possible. Both God and man have two names. The surname *Adam* refers to man's natural history, his past legacy and his involvement in an impersonal process; his first name, also *Adam* in this case, refers to his unique qualities as an individual, and points to the future. It is used to arouse him from his lethargy and summon him to his overarching human self. God also has two names. As *Elohim* He is the God of Nature who created the world and dispenses justice; as *Yahve* (the ineffable Name) He is the God of mercy who answers those who call upon Him in truth. The heresy of Marcionism holds that these two names refer to two different gods and that Jesus spoke only with the second. The Lord *our* God, however, is One and his *Name* is One.

This circumstance was understood by Adam for when, according to a traditional account, God, desirous of establishing closer relations with man, asked Adam to name Him (a request man could neither evade nor decline), Adam, quoting Scripture, complied:

Naming-Day in Eden

"It is fitting for Thee to be called *Adonai* since Thou art Lord of all Thy creatures, for it is written 'That is my name,' which means, that is the name by which Adam called me." This request was an immense concession on the Lord's part, for He was ordinarily loath to have His name revealed, preferring to appear under pseudonyms. But He had confidence in Adam as a name giver, for during the Review he gave names which have received universal approval. Years later when Moses inquired after the divine Name, he was rebuked by the Lord, who showed him His back parts. Pious commentators have taken this awkward passage as a lesson in divine instruction in the art of binding phylacteries to the back of the head. Despite this generous interpretation, however, the intent of the gesture is plain. Adam was the namer par excellence. He also gave himself a name: "It is fitting that I be called Adam because I come from the earth, *adamah*." This was Adam's first pun (Lat. *homo* from *humus*, earth, suggested by St. Isidore, would have been equally apt), and he seemed to be enjoying his role as namer.

Despite our rejection of the superstitious views of our benighted ancestors, we have not altogether discarded the belief in the virtue of names, except that our motives are more practical than moral. The sound and form of the names parents give to the newly born are not lightly negotiated and often rise to the heights of prophetic vision. If these names are found to be unsuitable in later life, they are frequently changed for business or social reasons and a name adopted which gives its owner an air of superior culture associated with the upper classes. A fruitful area of study for the student of the contemporary social scene is to be found in the name changing of immigrants, social climbers and cinema stars. This latter group, which occupies a prominent place in the public eye, might ponder the Freudian suggestion that it adopt names which lend themselves to erotic or slightly lewd connotations, perhaps names such as Joy, Bottome, Wetmore, Philpot, Bastert, Smalbehynd, and so forth.

The custom of changing names has been resorted to from time immemorial, although for reasons which appear to our practical age irrelevant. A number of biblical characters changed their names to correspond to the changed nature of their condition, as Abram to Abraham, Jacob to Israel, Naomi (*sweet*) to Mara (*bitter*). Pythagoreans were wont to exchange names in the belief that they would thus be able to share their mutual virtues. In Jewish tradition to this day the name of a person who is critically ill is sometimes changed in order to confuse the Angel of Death. For the same reason an infant born into a family in which other infants have been lost is left unnamed, being referred to as *Alter*, the old one, until after marriage, when he is given the name of one of the patriarchs. Some historical characters have received new names as a reward for some heroic exploit, as Siegfried or Victoria. Others had names bestowed upon them for some intellectual achievement, as some Hebrew authors in the Middle Ages who were named after the titles of their books: Joseph Caro was called Bet Josef and Jacob ben Asher became Baa'l ha-Turim. Famous men among the Greeks often received a nickname because of some distinguishing trait: Sophocles was known as *The Bee* because of the honeyed sweetness of his diction, Chrysostom as *The Light* because of his great learning, Chrysippus of Tarsus as *The Column of the Portico* because of the subtlety he displayed in the disputes at the Academy. This figure of speech, known as synecdoche, is a common form of appellation in the modern underworld, with an expected emphasis on the physical: *The Body, The Voice, Legs, Fingers, Greasy Thumb,* and so on. Synecdoche degenerates into tapinosis when an invidious or repugnant personal trait is made conspicuous by comparing a person to some base inanimate object which is calculated to detract from his dignity, as: *highbrow, egghead, sap, screwball, tightwad, battleax, ham, heel, scab, deadpan, wallflower.* The comic effect of these words is due to the excessive prominence given to the material and the inanimate over the spiritual.

The virtue of name punning, inaugurated by Adam, has persisted throughout the ages. Solemn inferences have been drawn from a pun on a name. The Bible takes special delight in such puns. The root meaning of Jacob is *heel* in the literal and in the slang sense, for Jacob emerged from the womb holding Esau's heel and later dished him out of his birthright. The Catholic Church is founded on the double meaning of the Greek name Peter. The most famous pun in literature is the one made by Ulysses when he outwitted Cyclops by calling himself *Noman.* Nor did a later age find name punning repugnant. It is a common form employed in the mottoes emblazoned on coats-of-arms. A chapel in Westminster Abbey which bears the name of Bishop Islip is adorned with a rebus showing an eye and a lad slipping from a tree, inscribed with the words "I slip." In two of his sonnets Shakespeare rings all the changes on his Christian name Will. Charles Lamb, for whom "a pun was as perfect as a sonnet," spoke of himself on one occasion as Lamb-punning (lampooning). The poet Donne outdoes himself with:

> When thou hast done, thou hast not done,
> For I have more. . . .
> And having done that: Thou hast done,
> I fear no more.

The addiction to punning is so ingrained in our nature that the noblest of men have not shrunk from playing with their names even on their deathbeds. The last defiant words of Huss at the stake were: "You may burn Huss [goose] now, but Luther [swan] will come." Rabelais found time before dying to deliver himself of the following: "Put me on my [*domino*] robe for I am cold;

besides, I would die in it" (Beati qui in *Domino* moriunter).
Thomas Hood, the most prolific of all the English punsters, had
the presence of mind *in articulo mortis* to concoct his last pun:
"Now the undertaker will earn [urn] a livelihood [lively Hood]."
Several irrepressible punsters, pressed for time, have had their
last witticism placed posthumously on their tombstones. Thus, the
tomb of a certain Mr. Knight bears the simple inscription "Good
Knight!" and the epitaph of a Mr. Partridge reads:

> What! kill a Partridge in the month of May!
> Was that done like a sportsman? eh, Death, eh?

Literary men are not averse to malicious or trivial punning.
Luther carelessly wrote the name of one of his numerous enemies,
Dr. Eck, as one word *Dreck* (filth). Disraeli was known to in-
timates as Dizzy and John Keats as Junkets. Stirling Coyne, the
great dramatist, was nicknamed Filthy Lucre. The feeble pun
"Anne ascended to the throne of her Anne-cestors" has been attributed to Hume. If the accusation is true, it is unworthy of the
great philosopher. No one stooped lower in this regard than
Dean Swift, who did not shrink from such mutilations as: seizer
(Caesar), laid a couple of eggs (Leda), kill ease (Achilles), airy
stuff (Aristophanes), and so on. English with its wealth of homonyms and haphazard spelling lends itself to such verbal enor-
mities. Writers are more scrupulous in choosing appropriate names
for the characters in their productions. Among the ancients Eu-
ripides was known as "the etymologizing tragedian" because of
his addiction to name punning. Ben Jonson, Racine, Smollett and
Gogol had an eye for the physical or moral peculiarities of their
characters, for whom they found apt names. But it was Charles
Dickens who, by the elaborate use of vowel symbolism, developed this art of name giving into a literary sophistication.
Thus, the short *i* in a name would denote a tender or timid quality
(Fips, Grig, Sniggs), the dark *u* solemn or clumsy traits (Muff,

Bumble, Buzfuz), the *u* plus the *i* a mixture of both (Nupkins, Spruggins). A descriptive name could be formed by prefixing a solitary consonant (Smangle), by omitting an initial letter (Crachit), by adding a suffix (Snagsby) or by merely changing a vowel sound (Drood, *dread*). Dickens ransacked birth and death records for suitable suggestions. His most genial invention was his name for Grandfather Smallweed, a gentleman who had to be beaten periodically, like a pillow, to have his human shape restored.

Formerly, names were given for sensible reasons. A physical trait, however unlovely, might suggest the infant's name: Oedipus (swell-foot), Boccaccio (big mouth), Calvin (bald), Varus (bowlegged), Crassus (fatty), Cincinnatus (curly), Cicero (chick pea), derived from an unpleasant excrescence on the Roman orator's nose. A name could be conferred because of some adventitious circumstance. Odysseus was so named because his grandfather Autolykos arrived at the christening "full of wrath"; Brutus received his name because he successfully escaped Tarquin's malignancy by affecting idiocy. Or, if small things may be compared to great, the name Noah (Heb. comfort) was appended to the author of these pages in honor of the Patriarch whose activities, as recorded in the early chapters of Genesis, constituted the required liturgical reading during the week of his birth. Such names, derived from apparently irrelevant circumstances, often express the wish that their literal meaning might be fulfilled or the hope that they may later prove to have been appropriately chosen. There are instances in history where the very reverse has happened. The bearer of the name Law swindled the government, Blunt was a man of uncommon sharpness and Boniface a fellow with an extraordinary amount of cheek. Edward Freely, the confectioner in George Eliot's *Romola*, had a generous-sounding name and yet was a man whose impulses were restrained and whose life was governed by the sound business principle "that the desire for sweets and pastries must only be satisfied in a direct ratio with the power to pay for them." Similarly, Erasmus Holiday, the schoolmaster in *Kenilworth*, owed his Christian name to a secret presentiment in his mother's mind that in the babe a hidden genius lay dormant which one day would lead him to rival the fame of the great scholar of Amsterdam; and he bore the surname Holiday, quasi *lucus a non lucendo*, as his students were inclined to think, because he granted so few holidays. Our own poet Tristram Coffin (lugubrious sarcophagus) is, *per antiphrasin*, the most incurable optimist in the profession.

A large number of names, however, have proved to be surprisingly apt. Consider the name Hammering Henry Armstrong, the pugilist who held three world boxing titles simultaneously! Repeat aloud the name Phineus P. Quimby, the watchmaker who cured Mary Baker Eddy! Could a *watchmaker* be more strikingly named? Not unless it were Thomas Tompion, the famous English clockmaker, in whose stately name we hear not only the ponderous tickings of the mute alliterative *t*'s but the chiming of the abrupt labial nasals as well. No wonder he was buried in Westminster Abbey! Then there are Titus Oates, a man of straw, who deserved to be thrashed, and a certain Dr. Tongue whose name fitted him to a *T*, for he was an uncommonly slippery fellow and always in a pickle. It seems that the gingival *T*, although a pure mute with no sound of its own, is excellent as the initial letter of famous names (Tacitus, Tintoretto, Turgeniev, Talleyrand, Torquemada and Torquato Tasso) and certain professions:

> It seems as if Nature had curiously planned
> That our name with our trades should agree.
> There Twining, the Tea-man, who lives in the Strand,
> Would be whining if robbed of his T.

The clearest case of predestination, however, is the name Rumhole, which belongs to the owner of a London pub.

31

Naming-Day in Eden

The character who has suffered most from the ravages of punning is, beyond all doubt, Ajax. In Sophocles' play by that name the hero in a desperate mood is driven to pun on his own name, which in Greek has the same sound as the common interjection of sorrow or woe:

> Ay me! Whoe'er had thought how well my name
> Would fit my misery? Aye me! Aye me!

It is an additional unfortunate circumstance that this Greek hero who died of vexation should bear a name that is phonetically equivalent to the older English word for privy. We still find it so used by Lear's Kent who, while scuffling with one of the servants, is moved to exclaim: "I will tread this unbolted villain into mortar, and daub the walls of a jakes with him." The word is now obsolete, and others have sprung up to replace it. But in former times when the word was current it captured the etymological imagination of ordinary folk for whom it called up the vision of an old man groaning on the toilet (Ajax = age aches). It is recorded that a certain Jaques Wingfield was overcautiously introduced in court as Privy Wingfield. This unfortunate similarity of sound induced Sir John Harington, the English translator of Ariosto, to write his famous *Metamorphosis of Ajax*, with an appendix bearing the title *Ulysses on Ajax*. The alleged purpose of this cloacinean satire, the first Rabelaisian specimen of which our language can boast, was to describe a species of water closet which the author had erected near Bath. Prurient readers who are diverted by such facetiae can find this stale subject refreshed by a contemporary writer, Reginald Reynolds, who in his book *Godliness and Cleanliness* duly acknowledges his debt to Harington. Ajax is the prototype of the bearers of punnable names. But we are all sensitive to our names and resent having them tampered with. Goethe in his *Autobiography* relates how as a young man he was infatuated with his own name, how he wrote it everywhere and how its very sound awed him and how he resented the clever plays on his name in a sonnet published by Friedrich Schlegel. This innocent raillery so irked Goethe that he rebuked the perpetrator in the following revealing words: "I dare say it was unseemly in him to permit himself a jest at the expense of my name. A man's name is not, as it were, a mantle thrown over his shoulders, that can be yanked and plucked at will. It is rather a perfectly fitting garment, nay, a veritable skin grown on him and which can be mutilated only with injury to the man himself."

The deliberate distortion of a name is often intended to harm the owner (Ibsenity, for example). Sometimes the name is used as an epithet and then gradually converted into a common noun. At first a name may be used to refer to some distinguishing trait, as: "Rousseau was the Newton of the ethical world"; "Thomas is but Aristotle sainted"; "Theodore Roosevelt was a combination of St. Paul and St. Vitus." Then the proper name may be emphasized by being repeated in a pregnant sense, a figure of speech called ploce, as: "In that battle Caesar was Caesar, Cicero continued to be Cicero," where the characteristic qualities of bravery and eloquence implicit in the respective names emerge. To names less known an adjective or qualifying phrase is appended, as: *a doubting Thomas, a dumb Dora, a simple Simon, a Holofernes of folly, a Gogmagog of nonsense.* If widely used, the name assumes the function of an adjective, as: *Melba toast, Sacher Torte, Molotov cocktail;* or, *Spinozan, Socratic, Dantesque, Platonist, Jacobite, Hobbist* or *Hobbian, Pepysian* (pronounced Peepsian) and *Shavian* (to rhyme with Fabian). Fictional characters have given us *Pickwickian, Pecksniffian, Micawberish* and *Shandean.* From the German we have *Wagnerian* and *Nietzschean* but Heine and Schopenhauer have resisted adjectival endings, as have the French names Rousseau and Montaigne. The Russians have succeeded in making an adjective of Mark Twain (*marktvénovski*)

33

and the Germans with less success a verb of Friedrich Nietzsche (*sich befriedrichnietzschen lassen*).

In the last stage of this hypostatization the salient quality in the word becomes dominant and assumes a separate existence as a generalized common noun written with a small letter, which may function also as an adjective or verb, its origin all but forgotten. Thus, we have the nouns *dunce* (Duns Scotus), *saxophone* (Adolphe Sax of Belgium), Fr. *gringalet*, a shrimp of a man (from Gringalet, a clown of the seventeenth century), *sadism* (Marquis de Sade, born 1740, infamous for his crimes and the character of his writings), *masochism* (Leopold von Sacher-Masoch, Austrian novelist, who described this affliction); common nouns from the Bible: *simony, onanism, jezebel;* animal names derived from proper nouns: *jackdaw* (Jack), *rabbit* (Robert), *magpie* (Margaret), *parrot* (diminutive of Peter); proper names transferred to the names of flowers: *begonia* (Bégon, governor of Santo Domingo), *dahlia* (Andreas Dahl, Swedish botanist), *camellia* (Josef Kamel, a Jesuit priest), *lobelia* (Matthias de L'obel, Flemish scholar), *gloxinia* (B. P. Gloxin, German botanist), *zinnia* (J. G. Zinn, professor of medicine at Göttingen); adjectives derived from the gods of mythology: *jovial, mercurial, saturnine, venereal, aphrodisiac, protean, erotic;* the verbs *hector, out-herod, bowdlerize, tantalize;* adjectives derived from fictional characters: *quixotic, gargantuan, euphuistic, dryasdust;* and words of saintly origin: *maudlin* (Magdalene), *nickel* (St. Nicolaus), *dago* (St. Diego), *maumet* (Mohammed), *tawdry* (St. Audrey), *petrel* (St. Peter), *pantaloons* (St. Pantaleone), *cereal* (the Roman goddess Ceres, protector of crops), *opportune* (Portunus, the Roman god of ports), and *ladybug* (bug of our Lady).

This scrupulous concern for fitting names is not shared by most men today. We tend to regard a name as an arbitrary designation, simply a meaningless mark which enables it to be made the subject of discourse, but which in no way indicates the attributes belonging to the bearer. A proper name is a word which identifies its object by virtue of its sound alone, unassisted by considerations of associated meanings. The mind is stopped by the sensible externals of sound before it could arrive at the meaning. Wellington did not conquer India because of his resonant, aggressive name. Had Napoleon borne the cognomen Klotz or had George Washington sustained the appellation Izod Flopson, those unamiable names would now be uttered with reverence. Is Klopstock, the German Milton, too dull a name to resound through the ages? Fame does not love only high-sounding names. Those who hold this "convention theory" are impervious to the fascination of names.

An extreme measure in this direction was taken in ancient Greece by Diodorus who defiantly called his slaves by the names of the Greek particles. A name is a label, and there is no necessary correspondence between it and its owner—an evil person can have a beautiful name, as Delilah; or an ugly name, as Jezebel; and good people can have beautiful names, as David; or ugly names, as Habakkuk. To those who cannot resist reading their prejudices into names, who strive to discover the workings of the mind in the physiognomy of a name and fancy they see angles in Izaak Walton's face, Paulus Silentiarius directed his bitter epitaph:

> My name, my country—what are they to thee?
> What, whether base or proud, my pedigree?
> Perhaps I far surpassed all other men,
> Perhaps I fell below them all; what then?
> Suffice it, stranger! that thou seest a tomb;
> Thou know'st its use; it hides—no matter whom.

 VI *The Bridal Procession*

An ancient interpretation of the Naming Scene in Eden has it that the animals were paraded before Adam so that he might choose one of them as his wife. The naming of the animals was not the primary purpose of the Review. God could have named them Himself, as He did the luminaries and the natural phenomena in the first chapter of Genesis. The parade was in reality God's way of selecting a mate for first man. The beasts that filed past Adam, then, were prospective brides submitting themselves to his inspection. The interjection of dissatisfaction with which he indicated their inadequacy constituted the act of naming. The linguistic machinery that Adam had put into motion on that occasion was not designed to reduce his experiences to a communicative, cognitive form but to express his own subjective taste and personal values; that is, to give vent to the disturbing affections which the dumb, faceless beasts evoked in him. The reaction of his motor impulses was central, and the cognitive object remained conspicuously nude. The beginning of human speech is to be found in the interjection, the natural cry, in which thought is identified with the acoustic vehicle of sound. Thus, the sound of the *u* would stand for melancholy, *i* for the blue of heaven, *ä* for yellow, *ö* for brown, and so forth, according to an elaborate table of *Lautsymbolik* known as "Romantic synesthesia." The word *cuckoo* would at first denote the emotion which the call of this bird awakens and only later would the emotional element disappear from this interjection and leave the pure sign. In short, language is fundamentally an affective activity whose prime intention is not communication but an unburdening of seething emotions, an activity which promotes the health of the nervous system. The names Adam gave were not objective descriptions of the objects before him but constituted an emotional workout in self-expression. This forgotten homiletical account of the Review anticipated by many centuries the modern neural theory of language, the interjectional or so-called pooh-pooh theory, although the latter cloaks its positivistic bias in scientific jargon while the former is animated by exegetical zeal. The tradition derives its conclusion from the circumstance that the very same verse in which Adam names the animals concludes with: "but for man there was not found a help meet unto him."

With what expletives did Adam announce his rejection of the eligible prospects? It is commonly agreed that he expressed his feelings in the natural exclamations of impatience and disgust common to all men and still in vogue today, that is, with sounds formed by compressing the lips as if chasing away a bad odor attacking the nostrils, somewhat less violent than the Bronx cheer: Eng. *tut, pshaw, fie, ugh* (which is the inarticulate sound of a hollow cough; Ger. *Pfui;* Norw. *pytt;* Heb. *tuff;* Welsh *ffei;* Fr. *zut;* Sp. *tate;* Hung. *csitt;* Russ. *tsits.* Actual words used as exclamations developed later, for example, *fiddlesticks, poppycock, eyewash* or *my foot.* With these or similar interjections Adam indicated his displeasure in the proposed left-handed matches. For a person of his exalted station to condescend to a morganatic union with one of the lowly creatures he had subjugated was an affront to his dignity. Had God meant him for such a disparaging (in the original sense of disparate) union, He would have left him to roam the forests on all fours and not have made him a master of languages (seven hundred in number, of which, according to Al-Kissai, Arabic was the most excellent). It is disconcerting to contemplate the striking modifications in our nature had first man's extravagant ardor, misguided by some momentary fever, preferred a scandalous mésalliance with one of the furry strangers. Human fancy has pictured such a commingling of the animal and the human in the imaginative creations of satyrs, centaurs, harpies, sirens, sphinxes and werewolves. Better to take a vow of sacerdotal celibacy and remain "a eunuch for the kingdom of Heaven" than stoop to such an indignity! But Adam had no taste for virginity. Marriage as corruption and fornication was a later theological development. Adam anticipated within him the first commandment, "Be fruitful, and multiply" (Genesis 1:28), for which he needed a spiritual spouse, meet unto him. For a spirit of melancholy, unknown to the animals, had begun to settle upon him. With all his symbolic know-how, he was suffering from boredom. His mental superiority and the spectacular results of his linguistic exploits had only served to insulate him from the rest of creation. This was at once the source of his material blessings and spiritual poverty. For although he had dominion, he had no romance. He strutted about listening to the reverberations of his own tender monologues. It cannot be said that he was solitary, for he did not yet know the meaning of society or sin. He was just miserable—no one to talk to, to astonish or charm. In short, he was Eveless, or to use the quaint paronomasia of a modern critic, "Adam missed his missus."

The Lord recognized Adam's plight and, yielding to his persuasive arguments, recorded in the delightful medium of verse in the eighth book of Milton's great epic, He proceeded to fashion Eve. To this end He caused a deep sleep to descend upon Adam who, exhausted by the exertions of his first morning, was now lying on the green lawn "bathed in a balmy sweat." While he was immersed in anesthetic slumber, the Lord "stole" a rib from his

sinister side (the third rib, the crookedest) "which rarely He re-
fined/ And thereof made the mother of mankind." The word
stole is to be understood, according to the traditional version,
only in the sense of a thief who comes in the night, steals a silver
jug and leaves a gold one in its stead. Yet God had some misgivings, for he foresaw the nuisance Eve would turn out to be, and
He formed her hastily, incomplete (according to Freud) in a
significant detail compared to man, an irremediable defect which
fills her with envy. That woman was made of a rib is not to be
taken literally, for after the operation Adam still had all his ribs
intact. *Rib* is to be understood not in a material but in a figurative
sense as the most valuable part of a man. In Eskimo folklore, which
considers the thumb as the strongest and most valuable part of the
body, woman is created from man's thumb. The extreme negative
point of view with regard to woman's esthetic construction has
been stated by Mencken, who studied the problem at firsthand;
namely, that in comparison with woman the average milkjug or
even cuspidor is an object of gratifying design. Yet, with all her
blemishes God made woman the object of man's rapture, and
implanted in the female bosom the means of his redemption.

The stage was now set for the great drama of Life, which was
to enjoy a long run until the end of time. The protagonist had
already made his appearance on the green stage, reciting monologues. The Devil was lurking in the wings awaiting the entrance
of his stooge, the *janua diaboli*, who had just been formed. The
actors had no prepared script and felt uncertain about their im-
provisations. But they were highly accomplished and ideally
suited for the roles they were to enact. The stagehands had just
finished putting the props in place and setting the traps. And
now the curtain went up on a thrilling succession of dramatic
scenes which some have found entertaining, others exasperating
and still others a tale told by an idiot, full of sound and fury,
signifying nothing.

 VII *Adam Introduces Himself*

When the last and fairest of God's works entered upon the scene, Adam straightway established her identity with the ecstatic tristich: "This time it is bone of my bone and flesh of my flesh." The words "this time," being of the feminine gender in the original, are taken to indicate Adam's approval, equivalent to: "Now, that's more like it!" or, "That fills the bill!" The Hebrew word for *time* (*pa'am*) also happens to mean *bell*, whose clanging suggested to Adam the name Eve (Heb. *ḥvh*, talk), mother of all speaking things. An excellent name—short, reversible and easily articulated even by the dentally defective. Time did not reduce it to a common noun, like *abigail* or degrade it to a harridan, like *jezebel*. It has resisted the decapitation of German names, Lotte (Charlotte), Gretchen (Margareta), or the caudal mutilation of the English Dotty, Maggie, Gertie. Above all, it does not lend itself to promiscuous punning, as for example Petrarch's Laura: *l'aura*, breeze; *l'auro*, gold; *lauro*, laurel. Nor did Adam exploit an adventitious, arbitrary circumstance as poets who often choose names for reasons of sound alone. One has a "passion for Mary for it calls up the realms of fairy"; for another

Adam Introduces Himself

Helen is fairer than the evening star, though *Hell* is in her name and a hell she was to men. The complete dependence of thought to the artifice of rhyme is to be found on the epitaph of a spinster:

> Beneath these high Cathedral stairs
> Lie the remains of Susan Pares;
> Her name was Wiggs, it was not Pares,
> But Pares was put to rhyme with stairs.

In the actual affairs of daily life, particularly in the delicate matter of choosing a mate, poets have been known to compromise with harsh reality and to disregard the sound of a name, and even the name itself. Oliver Goldsmith records that he chose *his* wife caring neither for her name or looks but selected her "as she did her wedding-gown, not for a fine glossy surface, but for such qualities as would wear well," and soberly adds that "for pickling, preserving and cookery, none could excel her." This practical attitude is generally not associated with the ethereal tone of poets, although it never leaves the mind of the beloved:

> I asked my fair one happy day,
> What I should call her in my lay,
>   By what sweet name from Rome or Greece:
> Lalage, Neaera, Chloris,
> Sappho, Lesbia or Doris,
>   Arethusa or Lucrece.
>
> "Ah!" replied my gentle fair,
> "Beloved, what are names but air?
>   Choose thou whatever suits the line:
> Call me Sappho, call me Chloris,
> Call me Lalage or Doris,
>   Only, only call me Thine."
>
>   —Lessing's *Namen*,
>   translated by Coleridge

Naming-Day in Eden

Now that Eve had a name, Adam could greet her. But the name itself did not reveal relevant details which he had a right to know. He knew her only in a social sense, as a nodding acquaintance. To open a way for further knowledge he could have adopted two extreme positions—on the one hand, to indulge in introverted reflection and self-deception and on the other, to resort to peeping and eavesdropping. Both methods, however, are unsatisfactory, for they fail to yield the *reciprocal* knowledge necessary to social intercourse among equals. It was at this juncture in the history of the world that Adam made the momentous decision to surrender his anonymity and address Eve. For this he needed a complete, well cemented sentence, a thing thus far unattempted in prose or rhyme. The names he had given the animals, who wander about by instinct, were isolated and detached, forming a haphazard world of particularities without context or rhythm, without relational structure or logical coherence, unrelated pieces of clothing, as it were, upon a non-existent clothesline. To reach out to Eve, however, and draw her to him he needed a "line," that is, an artistic, literary objectification of an inner attitude. Now for the first time language came into its own, its spectacular social role. The monologue of the solitary reflective thinker now gave way to a dialogic discussion, involving the art of listening, the risk of contradiction and cross-examination and a shift from egotism to tuism. Ventriloquism gave way to corroboration as the criterion of truth. Ultimate values were no longer derived from subjective certainty, but from loyalty to similar principles based on consent and compromise. Adam's world ceased to be the object of solitary contemplation and became a field of concern and responsibility.

Happily unaware of the magnitude of the enterprise and its fateful implications, but filled with a sense of vague felicity, Adam now turned to Eve and with graceful levity introduced himself with the sentence, "Madam, I'm Adam"—the earliest instance, if we can rely on an old account, of a palindrome, that is, a phrase that reads the same whether read backward or forward. This intricate figure is also known as *versus diabolici*, for the Devil is said to have concocted it and then to have whispered it to Adam. Its diabolical character lies in its circular form which denies the irreversibility of time. This seems to defy common sense. Eggs cannot be unscrambled. The moving finger writes and, having writ, moves on. Our lives evolve in one direction, from seed to fruit, from child to adult, from temptation to victory, and not vice versa. God sees us but we cannot see Him. Yet, with a religious instinct for the absurd, Adam divined the secret of this mystical circularity implicit in the palindrome. Blunders *can* be undone and the consequences of an act erased by penance; the past *can* be re-collected and lost things recovered, even lost innocence. The Fall, as Adam was yet to learn, was painful but not irreparable. There *is* a road which leads back to Eden.

Adam's introduction was a simple *ad rem* declaration of his personal identity. It was not a boastful battology, the erudite twaddle of a Dr. Adam, indicating the speaker's profession, income and social station. Good breeding does not permit such intrusive details in early courtship, *a fortiori* such insolent subterfuges, as: "Haven't we met before?" "Do you speak English?" "Can I buy you a drink?" or "Have you seen my etchings?" Adam's consciousness of his mental superiority did not prompt him to forego polite behavior. At the same time he did not indulge in the trite formulas of self-disparagement, making excuses for his rustic origin, lack of higher education, the inadequate grasp of the subject matter or the "being unaccustomed to public speaking." The art of conversation demands that we avoid becoming involved in discussions of serious problems or personal opinions. In the symbolic play of conversation concrete content must remain undetermined and transported to the airy realm of

43

form for the sake of sociability. Argumentative showdowns with women are in poor taste. It mistakes women for rational creatures to be convinced with logic instead of emotional creatures to be placated and, if possible, loved.

Adam, therefore, made no attempt to elenchize Eve or to impress her with baculine arguments. He proceeded in accordance with the philosophical principle laid down by his namesake Adam Smith, a forgotten philosopher, who reduced all ethics to a matter of good breeding, which consists in not burdening others with our intellectual or orectic conflicts and in suppressing our personal feelings which, however tormenting to us, cannot be expected to affect our neighbor. Such an attitude is not an original instinct in man; it is a social product artificially acquired. How amazing it is, then, that Adam, bereft of the refining influences of social intercourse and the redeeming discipline of domestic life, should have been acquainted with the polite observances of modern etiquette! On what authority was his deportment based? There was no law at the time to inhibit rude expressions of primitive feelings. Adam had before him no approved models of moral conduct. And yet he extricated himself from a delicate predicament with a verbal flourish, which adds immensely to his reputation as a man of the world as well as a linguist. It would seem that good taste in social matters is an original faculty rooted in a generous nature independent of traditional codes. Adam's chivalrous behavior on this occasion, his delicate sentiments, his *savoir faire* and *je ne sais quoi* (we are obliged to borrow these tender terms from the French because the spirit of chivalry was formerly interwoven with the texture of French manners) have induced some erudite authors, chiefly French, to conclude that the French language must have been the idiom of our Parents in Eden. It should be recalled, however, that (men being what they are) Adam's chivalry did not compromise his sense of personal safety when he turned State's witness against his helpmate in the scandal which erupted later in the day.

A small but significant feature in Adam's singular introduction is his use of the personal pronoun *I*. With only two people in the world Eve could not possibly have known that *I* was not Adam's proper name, for she had not heard how each person refers to himself as *I* but is not called *I* by others. With many people speaking, Eve would have noted that *I* refers to the speaker, that is, to the subject *and* the object of speech, and *Thou* to the subject spoken to *and* the object of speech. But with only one other person in the world, Eve could not be expected to arrive of herself to such a high degree of abstraction. Hence, Adam plainly told her, "*I'*m Adam." To this *I* which posited the existence of his personal being (following Descartes), Adam was careful to prefix the vocative *Madam* in order to acknowledge the existence of the objective world (after Aquinas). The entire phrase, when delivered with assurance, has the obvious connotation: "This earth (*adamah*) belongs to me, Adam, by rights of dominion and etymology. I had you under my skin but I asked to have you externalized so that you could share this home with me." This direct declaration of possession is more honest than the Spanish "Está Usted en su casa!" (This is your house!), which is said to a guest on entering a Spanish home. This bizarre phrase is, of course, a mere *façon de parler* in which language has ousted sense, and if interpreted literally would lead to confusion and disaster. The immodest but honest tone of Adam's declaration is symbolized by the arrogant perpendicular *I* (the dominative case) which is capitalized only in English whereas the German and the Spanish capitalize the *you* (*Sie; Usted*). In this personal pronoun foreign critics detect a pretentiousness altogether out of proportion to its feeble sound and ample proof, if any is needed, of the ingrained immodesty of the English character. The French *je* is more adaptable and gregarious, often losing part of itself in

45

its neighbor. The solitary Hebrew *ani* has maintained itself intact only in the present tense. The Russian Я, to judge from its shape, is a solitary, gaping, frivolous letter. The German *ich*, of course, is the most harmonious and audacious; it is internally related to its accusative *mich*, as *je* is not to *moi* nor *I* to *me* (the objectionable case), and hence can play with itself eternally, as it does in Fichte's philosophy.

In his manner of delivery Adam showed more than an elementary knowledge of acoustics and phonetics. The four *a*'s of the palindrome were properly chosen for open-air delivery, and their quick succession must have shaken Eden's bower. Failure to sandhize the third *a* in *I'm* (*sandhi* is the technical term taken from Hindu grammar for such elided forms) would have resulted in a uniform distribution of an equal number of vowels and consonants, and this would have betrayed a cynical indifference on Adam's part to an inherently dramatic encounter. For in normal speech there are four times as many consonants as vowels, corresponding to the relation between breathing and blood circulation (eighteen breaths to seventy-two pulse beats). Fine shades of emotion are hence indicated by a judicious mixture, a dramatic situation requiring a preponderance of ephemeral feminine vowels over the more enduring masculine consonants. As it is, the five vowels and six consonants of the palindrome are ideally combined to indicate the desired relation between the effective lyrical elements and the cognitive content. Adam's hankering after *m*'s (mimmation), which constitute more than one-third of the letters, belongs to the infancy of speech as well as to the speech of infancy, for it is the labial noise of oral gratification made by a sucking babe, a circumstance which has led psychologists to look for the origin of human speech in man's sexual activities. The succession of this homoioteleuton of *m*'s threatens to reduce the entire phrase to an incoherent mumble were it not supported at both ends by the defensive *d*'s, which, being formed in front of the mouth by the extended tongue, express assent and gratitude. The *d* is the altruistic letter par excellence (*dar, donner, davat, didomi, danke, Dieu*), and hence the two *d*'s which detained Adam's slipping tongue indicate that he gave generously and without reserve. Since then the *d* has disappeared from *gospel* (OE *godspel,* good spell) and *gossip* (OE *godsibb,* God's kinsman, godfather, chum) and found its way into *scoundrel* (Scot. *skunner* or *scowner*).

The jubilant delivery of the introduction is somewhat dimmed by the *l* sound (the universal sound of woe) at the very heart of the phrase, a foreboding that all was not well, but fortunately it remains unemphasized in its contracted sandhized form. Even a momentary indecision at this point would have thrown Adam back into formlessness. The slightest change in phraseology would have been fatal to his intention. Had he halted during the delivery as if unable or unwilling to proceed (aposiopesis) and abandoned his original construction for another (anacolouthon) or feigned to conceal his real meaning (apophasis), his communication would have been irreparably disrupted. The emotional inversion "Am I Adam, Madam?" would have introduced doubts at the very outset; "Adam, that's me, Madam!" is vulgar and defiant; "I am Adam, Madam!" gains a parechesis but loses the sandhi and, as all the other alternate forms, the palindrome to boot.

Nor did Adam sing his introduction as many researchers, including Jespersen, insist (the hi-de-ho theory). Although Adam was careful to exclude harsh sounds from his introduction (the wild *r*'s and *k*'s, the explosive *p*'s and the anxious vowel *u*), he did not burst into song. He spoke the phrase *con amore,* in a clear, unconstipated voice, undamaged by excessive beer drinking. Singing reduces thought to sound, subordinates the idea to the tone and the meaning to the music. Adam's knowledge of acoustics and phonetics, however useful, did not engage the central powers of his mind. The ultimate end of his eloquence was not esthetic form but moral fervor. This is evident in the arrangement of Adam's pauses after the vocative, before the personal pronoun and a final pause after his name to indicate that the utterance was finished and that the intended sense of the sentence was completed. The breaths were not taken regularly or at random but were consciously directed to significant pauses corresponding to a sensible division in the thought expressed. It is impossible to talk without breathing (eighteen to twenty-two times a minute) for it is a biological necessity to exchange stale for fresh air. But this vital compulsion of inhaling was attached by man to human speech and made subservient to a superior principle of social communication.

In this first social utterance, then, Adam gave evidence of his ability as a linguist (with his dextrous palindrome and its phonetic finish), as a psychologist (with his use of the personal pronoun, his tact and restrained delivery) and above all as a moralist (by subjecting his desultory fancy to method and his enthusiasm to self-control). Communication was his first concern. Yet, as an exegete and a poet the importance of the sound and shape of words and their constituent letters did not escape him—a subject which will be pursued in the following chapter.

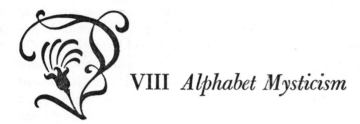

VIII *Alphabet Mysticism*

The visual interpretation of single letters finds its most elaborate treatment in what is known as "alphabet mysticism." This is a realm dear to the mystics who often receive their inspiration from the esoteric meaning disclosed by the form of a letter. When a word is spelled, that is, broken up into its constituent letters, its spell is broken and the meaning locked up within it is released. The mind is thus set free from the lure of sound and delivered from the idolatry of the spoken word. Here the sound killeth, but the letter, if stared at long enough, redeemeth. In the Islamic tradition, which holds calligraphy in high regard, God revealed the letters of the alphabet, as well as the spoken word, to Adam. In the Jewish tradition this revelation is reserved for Moses, who learned the alphabet from the Tables of the Law during the forty days he spent on the mountaintop. The orthodox hold that even the minute Hebrew vowel points were included in the revelation and have assailed as heretics those who have impugned their divine origin, as did Raymundus Martinus in *Pugeo Fidei* in the thirteenth century, followed by Zwingli, Grotius and Cotton Mather, who wrote his M.A. thesis at Harvard on this very subject.

The most elaborate exegetical use of alphabet symbolism was

made by Rabbi Akiba who reigned supreme in this fanciful realm. In his *Crowns of the Letters* he explains every horn, apex, crown and virgula with which the Hebrew letters are adorned. He relates that when the Lord was about to create the world, the various letters of the alphabet competed for the honor of beginning the first verse of the Bible. The second letter was finally chosen on the ground that it is the first letter of the verse "Blessed is he who comes in the name of the Lord." Moreover, it is closed on one side to indicate the creation *ex nihilo* and open to the world on the other (ב). The first letter, the *aleph*, brought suit against the Lord, who acknowledged the justice of its case and promised to make it the first letter of the Decalogue. This method lends itself to homiletical purposes. For example, the superfluous dot on the letter *shin* (שׁ) in the verse where Esau kisses his brother preserves the dent of his tooth as he bit into Jacob's neck, which at that moment turned into marble. Why is the *yod* (י), the smallest letter in the Hebrew alphabet, the prefix of the future conjugation? To show that he who makes himself small will inherit the world to come.

This method was not confined to Talmudists. It was pursued with equal zeal by the enlightened Greeks to whom it was known by the name of *hopsis*, which may be defined as the esthetic delight derived from the shape of letters. In his *Cratylus* Plato discusses in great detail the forms and symbolic values of the various Greek letters, the *o* being round in shape and in sound, the *i* thin, and so on. Simonides is said to have invented the ω because of its resemblance to shadows, the ψ because of its similarity to the whistling arrow and the ξ because it looked and sounded to him like a saw. The letter γ was the symbol among the Greeks for the crossroads of decision; ε turned on its face represented balances; Δ had lewd association and φ phallic resemblances. This verbal pastime is to be found later in Germany during the baroque period when the letters of the alphabet were given characteristic designations: *r* was called "the dog's head," *s* "the snake," *z* "the grasshopper," and so on. This led to the practice of putting appropriate pictures beside the letters in children's books, a custom which has persisted down to our day. No less a modern spirit than Bacon noted that "the trembling of the water hath resemblance with the letter *l*, the quenching of hot metals with the letter *z*, the snarling of dogs with the letter *r*, the noise of screeching owls with the letters *sh*, the voice of cats with the diphthong *eu*, the voice of the cuckoo with the diphthong *ou*, and the sound of strings with the diphthong *ng*."

Some letters or sounds have been found extremely offensive and have been treated with indifference and even hostility. Chinese and infants have an aversion for the *r*, for which they substitute an *l*, a defect known in Greek as *traulós*, in English as lallation or lambdacism. Alcibiades suffered from this speech ailment which Aristophanes later ridiculed in *The Wasps*. Napoleon's wife Josephine, being a Creole, also found this sound difficult to pronounce, and omitted it when she spoke French, saying *incoyable* for *incroyable*, and so on. For a time this defect was imitated by others and almost succeeded in removing this exciting sound from the French language. The Japanese, on the other hand, prefer the *r* to the *l*, which they find difficult, and in later Laconian we find the *s* changing to an *r*. The exaggerated rolling of the uvular *r* is called *grasseyer* in French. In Parisian society of the sixteenth century the *r* was also pronounced like a *z* (Pazi for Paris), an affectation known as *zézayer*, which has left its mark on the French language in such words as *chaise* for the former *chaire*. On the other hand, the *z* sound was banished from the grammar of Appius Claudius Caecus (born 312 B.C.) because it sounded to his sensitive ear like the hiss which passes through the teeth of a dying man. The Spaniards have softened this voiced fricative to *th* and the Germans pronounce it as a *ts*. The inability to pronounce the *s* sound is called *blaesitas*. This abused letter has been regarded with suspicion from the very beginning. It is omitted from the first pages of the Hebrew Bible, probably so as not to suggest Satan's name. Quintilian called it "the viper letter," and Pindar, who excluded it entirely from his odes, a bastard sound. Some Roman poets, notably Terence and Lucretius, omitted it before *l* and *p*. One incensed poet erased every *s* in the Odyssey and put a *t* in its place. *T*, in turn, which became the favorite letter of tyrants for it has the shape of the gallows and the cross, was sued in one of Lucian's dialogues for rape and usurpation by seven other letters of the alphabet. The resentment against the *s* was continued by Jean Paul who dropped it from the genitive singular of German masculine and neuter nouns in order to avoid excessive sibilation. It has also disappeared from the body of many French words, and its omission is indicated by a circumflex accent. The tendency now in Spanish is to lisp it and even to drop it altogether.

Writers who exclude from their literary productions certain letters for which they have conceived an active dislike are known as lipogrammatists or letter droppers. The great master of this art was Tryphiodorus, a Greek poet of the sixth century, all of whose works except one have been lost. This ingenious writer composed an *Odyssey* of twenty-four books, calling the first *Alpha* because, *lucus a non lucendo*, it had no *alpha* in it, the second *Beta* because it contained no *beta*, and so on. Similarly, the indefatigable Spanish dramatist Lope de Vega, conceiving a strong distaste for all vowels, expended great skill on the malicious labor of writing five novels, from which he omitted the letter *a* from the first, *e* from the second, *i* from the third, *o* from the fourth and *u* from the fifth. At the other extreme we find the pangrammatists who evince an indiscriminate preference for *all* the letters, which they sometimes contrive to crowd into a single verse (compare Ezra 7:21 in the Hebrew). A pangrammatic affectation is Hucbald's eclogue on baldness addressed to Charles the Bald, each of whose 146 lines begins with a *C* in honor of the king's name.

Among the modern poets, especially among the French sym-
bolists, we find those who associate certain letters with definite
colors and emotions. Some writers have grown exceedingly fond
of the angular *k*. Grimm considered this letter the best for re-
search, exploration and the beginning of questions. Kafka is drawn
to the *k*, and the names of many of his heroes contain it. The
k is the king of the consonants! It lends weight to a word. How
thin and uncongenial *rhetoric* and *picnic* look without the old
terminal *k*, how much nobler *Sokrates* and the *kategorical imperative* with it! It adds a dash of ferocity to *Afrika*. In the poetical
line "Her Lyrick feet may dance before the Arke" it is apparent
that the *k* makes the lady's feet more ponderous—for which, fortunately, the poet has made room by an increase in the size of the
L and a more spacious spelling of *Arke*. The father of the existentialists, Kierkegaard, fancied at times that he detected human characteristics in parts of speech or even punctuation marks. A glance
through his writings reveals the following specimens:

I am silent as a *dagesh* (a point inserted in the bosom of a
Hebrew consonant to fortify it, though itself not pronounced).

I feel shrunken as a *shva* (a vacillating Hebrew vowel).

I am as faint as a *shva;* I am as weak and forgotten as a
dagesh.

I feel like a letter printed backward in the line and as introverted as a *pronomen reflexivum.*

There are people whose position in life is like an interjection, without influence in the sentence; they are the hermits
of life, and at most take a case.

I am as reflexive as a pronoun.

A follower is not an *alpha intensivum* but an *alpha pri-
vativum.*

Our politicians are like Greek reciprocals which are want-
ing in the nominative singular and all the subjective cases;

they can only be thought of in the plural and in the possessive cases.

This stylistic device which imbues inanimate particles with personal traits is also to be found among novelists in the description of their characters:

> She is as barren as an exclamatory *O*.
> Her eyebrows were shaped like circumflex accents (hippocrepian).
> His mouth had the shape of a *V* (hypsiloid).
> Her legs were constructed like a pair of parentheses (lunulated).
> His legs were formed like the Russian letter *л*.
> His mustache had the form of a ragged *W*.
> He was headed straight as a *Z* for immortality.

The Latin grammatical terms curiously lend themselves to erotic interpretations, an ambiguity exploited by Latin writers: *solecism* (errors of structure), *metaplasm* (deviation from the grammatical norm), *degenerate anastrophe* (the inversion of normal word order), as well as the obvious *conjugation, conjunction, declension, interjection,* and so on.

Our sophisticated age is prone to smile at this bizarre treatment of the alphabet. But a pious mind sees in the slightest alteration of a letter consequences that can shake the universe. In the letters of the alphabet lie at once the glory that lifts us above the beasts and our tragedy, an insight aptly summed up by Louis Aragon in his poem bearing the title "Suicide":

A b c d e f
g h i j k l
m n o p q r
s t u v w
x y z

 IX *Eve's Answer*

A moment of silence followed Adam's momentous introduction, "Madam, I'm Adam." Much depended on Eve's answer. To respond properly she would have to understand not only the relational structure and pattern of Adam's inner speech, which would depend on the similarity of their native endowment, but also the individual forms of the language adopted for the occasion, which would depend on an arbitrary cultural convention. To take an analogy from chess: the two partners must agree on the internal system of ideal relationships that exist among the pieces and also on the diverse imaginative forms which the individual pieces assume. One naïve interpreter takes the view, in the face of universal experience, that on this occasion Eve refrained from replying and kept her peace. This is a gratuitous assertion and highly improbable, although it would have won the rapturous applause of generations of men. Silence on Eve's part would have been an indulgent reproach and not a fitting rejoinder to Adam's civil introduction. Being at bottom a sensible woman, Eve based her answer on Swift's advice to his contemporaries; namely: "If you want to gain the reputation of being a sensible person, you should be of the opinion of the person with whom for the time being you are conversing." Flattery must have a measure of verisimilitude and imitation. Her genius, therefore, blazed forth with the answer "Eve!"—paying Adam back in the same coin in a palindrome one-fourth the length of his.

The exchange of names now united the pair in the knowledge of a secret shared only by them. Vanity and hope kindled a feeling of self-esteem in Adam. He was now certain that Eve had understood his words and had even been able "to read between the lines." What he could not know, however, was whether her answer represented her true feelings, should she be inclined to suppress them. She could too easily detach her words from the mental state she might wish to conceal. The mobile word, unlike a blush or a hiccough, is an artificial instrument of communication and can be liberated from its physical context. The advantage of the linguistic symbol is that it gives man the freedom to direct it in accordance with his intention; the disadvantage is that it can be deliberately misleading. There is no way, for example, of knowing the female heart from the words of her mouth. Much practice has perfected this fine art of dissembling in women. She can sigh for Achilles while in the arms of Odysseus. Female dissembling, or the art of symbolic detachment, however, is not a mortal sin, according to Aquinas, but only a venial offense. It may even be laudable when the end in view is not inconsistent with charity as, for example, in the inventive mendacity of the mother of an unmarried girl. Adam thought he perceived a slight tincture of this frailty in Eve. She had decoded his message and entered into his thoughts but he could not know what was in the back of her mind. For this he would have to peer behind the verbal fig leaf for the deep unity of form and content which is to be found not in racial characteristics or in the universal subject matter of discourse but in the distinctive accents of a particular idiom, its tone, intonation and inimitable phonetic patterns.

It is difficult to simulate a foreign accent. Even individual sounds are not easily negotiated by a foreign tongue—the Arabic gutturals, the Portuguese nasals, the Danish glottal stops, the Turkish dotless *ï*, the Basque *r*, the Polish and Dutch *ui*, the four Gaelic *l*'s, the impure English vowels. A Greek cannot pronounce a *b*, an Arab a *p*, a German a *w*, a Russian an *h*, a Frenchman a *th*, and so on. Hence, accent is the most excellent shibboleth for detecting strangers in our midst. The Hebrew word *shibboleth*, meaning "an ear of grain," was first used (Judges 12) as a test word to distinguish the Gileadites from the fleeing Ephraimites, who were unable to pronounce the initial *sh* sound. This fatal defect resulted in 42,000 Ephraimites being slaughtered by the enemy "without reprieve, adjudged to death/ For want of well pronouncing shibboleth." The distinction between *sh* and *s* (the שׁ and the שׂ) could not at that time have been made by the eye, similar to our *sure* and *sugar*, for the Hebrew diacritical marks were not introduced until the sixth century of the common era. This sound being unknown to the Greeks, the Septuagint does not retain the word *shibboleth*, for which it substitutes *stákhus*, an ear of corn. History records a number of instances where slight dialectal differences have entailed grave consequences. When the Druses came to slay Ibrahim Pasha's troops, the Damascene soldiers were sifted from the Syrian by means of the test word *gamel*, which the latter could pronounce only with an initial soft *g* sound. During the Sicilian Vespers at Palermo, which began at the first stroke of the vesper's bell on March 31, 1282, the French, who are unable to pronounce the Italian *ch* sound, were made to betray themselves by being forced to repeat the Italian phrase *ceci e ciceri* and were then massacred. Twenty years later they met a similar fate in Flanders for not being able this time to repeat a Dutch password properly which contained the difficult *sch* sound.

Romantics love to dwell on these inimitable differences in languages, which they take as a true reflection of the unique history of the people who speak them. The national soul is locked up within the national language, the principal bond of its unity. The language of a people is, as it were, the national tapestry into which the habits, hopes and fears of its speakers are woven, every strand tinged with emotional associations. No word can be adequately rendered into a foreign tongue, for one cannot enter into the soul of another. This shifts the center of linguistics from the study of logic and universal grammar to esthetics and stylistics. Foreign works are translated, imitated or plagiarized for the sole purpose of nourishing the bloodstream of the national language. Since the common tongue is the main adhesive factor in the spiritual unity of the people, it is an act of disloyalty to speak another. Rival tongues or dialects are frowned upon and, if need be, suppressed. In the interest of national unity foreign words which had crept into the language are eliminated. Language purity and chauvinism go hand in hand and dumbness is inflicted on those who refuse to don the linguistic uniform of the country.

This Romantic view is a recurrent theme in the life of nations, particularly in Germany where it was no small factor in isolating that country from the philosophic tradition of the West. It has its roots in the theory that language is the unique product of the collective national mind (Durkheim) and common soul (Herder) of its citizens who are the makers of history (Le Bon) and creators of law (Savigny), whose thought is infinite (Descartes) and instincts pure (Rousseau). We find the theory plainly set forth in Fichte's *Speeches to the German Nation:* each country has a spiritual task allotted to it by Providence, and Germany's task of redeeming mankind is to be carried out by all those who speak the German tongue, for German is "an heroic language" undiluted by foreign admixture. Political boundaries should be made to coincide with linguistic frontiers. Philology becomes a branch of anthropology and the handmaiden of politics. The tongue rather than the shape of the skull is made the criterion of nationhood. Man's allegiance is literally tested by lip service.

Each country has its Fichte, for each believes that what belongs to it is the best: *suum cuique pulchrum*—its causes the most righteous and its language the most elegant. Galen was of the opinion that Greek was by far the most elegant language and that those who spoke other tongues grunted, squealed or croaked. Charles V held that Spanish should be spoken to the gods, French to men, Italian to the ladies, German to soldiers, English to geese, Hungarian to horses and Bohemian to the Devil. One writer proved that the Devil seduced Eve in Italian, Eve misled Adam in Bohemian, the Lord scolded them both in German and the angel Gabriel drove them forth in Hungarian. A Persian writer has the serpent speak Arabic since it is the most persuasive language, Gabriel Turkish since it is the most menacing and Adam Persian since it is the language of love. For Diderot French was the best organized and the most precise language because it retains less than any other the lispings of the childhood of the race, adding his belief "that if Truth would return to earth, French would be her chosen speech." The love of our own is an elementary form of narcissism or nosism, and forms the most powerful ingredient in the love of family and country:

> The shuddering tenant of the frigid zone
> Boldly proclaims that happiest spot his own;
> Extols the treasures of his stormy seas,
> And his long nights of revelry and ease.
> The naked negro panting at the line,
> Boasts of his golden sands and palmy wine,
> Basks in the glare, or stems the tepid wave,

Naming-Day in Eden

> And thanks his gods for all the good they gave.
> Such is the patriot's boast, where'er we roam,
> His first, best country ever is at home.
> —Goldsmith, "The Traveller"

Patriotism in its negative forms leads to xenophobia, the hatred of foreigners. The linguistic expression of xenophobia is ethnophaulism, that is, the casting of aspersions on other nationalities and the imputation of unpleasant attributes to foreigners, usually behind their backs. The first imputation is that of unintelligibility of all tongues that we do not happen to speak. In German *deutsch* is related to *deutlich*, clear, and to *bedeutend*, significant. The word *gibberish* is derived either from *Egyptian*, from the Arabic *algarabia* (Fr. *charabia* = nonsense) or from an Arab alchemist Geber (compare Scott's *Kenilworth*, Chapter XI). *Bohemian* acquired its derogatory sense from the erroneous belief among the French that the gypsies came from Bohemia, and *gyp* from our belief that they came from Egypt (Pol. *szygan*, gypsy = swindler). We characterize unintelligible speech by saying, "That's Greek to me," the Russians and the Rumanians by "That's Chinese to me," the French by "That's Hebrew to me," the Germans by "That's Spanish to me," and the Poles by "I'm listening to a Turkish sermon." Those who are not fortunate enough to speak our tongue are dubbed dumb: the Slavs call the Germans *nemets*, dumb, and the Macedonian Turks call the Slavic Mohammedans *dilsyz*, tongueless. Even an imperfect knowledge of our tongue or an outlandish accent is censured: Heb. *loazim* = foreigners or stammerers; Fr. *bretoner* = to speak like a Breton or to stammer; Syr. *loäz* = to speak Egyptian, that is, to speak poorly; Dan. *tydska* = to talk German or gibberish; Ger. *welschen* (Welsh) = to speak German with an Italian or French accent; Ger. *Kauderwelsch* = thieves' jargon; Span. *vasconcear* = to speak Basque or to jabber; Fr. *parler français comme une vache espagnol* = to speak French as a Basque speaks Spanish (*vache,* cow, is a corrupt form of *Basque*). In German the derogatory morphological suffix *eln* indicates impure speech: *französeln,* to speak German with a French accent; *jüdeln,* to speak German with a Yiddish accent. A foreign word is generally preferred when a disparaging sense is desired: Ger. *räsonnieren,* to split hairs (from the French); Ger. *pleite,* bankrupt (from the Hebrew); Pol. *szachrajastwo,* to swindle (from Ger. *schachern,* which comes from Heb. *sakhar,* profit); Hung. *vigeč,* vagabond (from Ger. *wie geht's*); Russ. *šval,* a slicker (from Fr. *cheval* horse).

Foreigners are sometimes called by the names of their favorite foods: the Germans refer to the Italians as *Macaroni* and to the Jews as *Knoblauch* (garlic); we call the French *frogs,* the Rumanians call the Bulgarians *onions and garlic* (*ceapă si usturoi*), the Greeks *blue herrings* (*țăr*) and are themselves known as *mamaligari* (from corn cake, *mamaliga*). Or, a foreigner often receives a disparaging nickname derived from some recurrent word or phrase in his halting speech or from some characteristic phrase of his own language which strikes the native ear: we refer to the Spanish as *Spics* (from their *No "spic" English*); *Hottentot* is derived from *hot-en-tot,* the Dutch imitation of the native speech; the English were known in many countries as *godams* or *godons* (from the most common words heard in sailors' oaths), in Japan as *damuraisu H'to* (damn-your-eyes folk), in China as *a-says;* in Java a Frenchman was formerly known as an *orang-deedong* (*orang* = man, plus Fr. *dis-donc*) and in Spain as a *didon* for the same reason, in Australia as a *wi-wi* (Fr. *oui, oui*), in England as a *parlez-vous* and in Russia as a *šaramužnik* (Fr. *cher ami*).

We take it for granted that our language is the most natural mode of expression and we look upon others with tolerant amusement if not hostility. This is illustrated in the humorous dialogue on the French language between Huck and Jim in *Huckleberry*

Finn (end of Chapter XIV). A similar dialogue, not so well known, occurs in Gogol's *Marriage* between Anutchkin and Zhevakin:

A. Permit another question, sir: What language do they speak?

Z. All speak French in Sicily, naturally.

A. Really, every young lady speaks French!

Z. No exception. You'll hardly believe it—it sounds strange, but we stayed here thirty-four days, and in all that time we didn't hear a word of Russian. Think of it!

A. Not a word?

Z. Nary a word. And I'm not thinking of their noblemen and signors and other such officers of theirs. Just take the common man there, some filthy fellow that carries about all kinds of stuff on his neck and just say to him: "Give me some bread, good man," and he won't understand you—I swear to you, he won't. But tell him in French! "Dateci del pane" or "Portate vino" and he'll get it for you, sure enough, and he'll run and fetch it right, every time.

Our language is clear and meaningful, and we are startled when others do not find it so. Those who speak a foreign tongue are for the Greeks "barbarians"—the iterated syllables of this natural onomatopoeia still linger in the Eng. *babble,* Sp. *balbucear,* Arab. *barbar,* Fr. *balbal.* The term in Greek at first implied neither hostility nor disrespect, but merely indicated the jibber-jabber of foreigners, somewhat in the manner in which we regard the Chinese. Thus, the Persian ambassador in Aristophanes' *The Acharnians* is called "barbarian" because of his strange speech. When Agamemnon in Sophocles' *Ajax* rebukes Teucer for being a barbarian, the latter retorts in a surprisingly modern fashion: "If you go back far enough, you will find that there is no such thing as racial purity. What about your grandfather, Pelope, who was the son of Tantalus, a Phrygian of Asia Minor?" Generally, however, the word *barbarian* was used reproachfully. This is in keeping with views of Aristotle (the father of the scientific method!), who described the differences between the Greeks and the barbarians as inherited, inevitable and rooted in nature. However, it was not until the rise of nationalism and democracy that we find ethnophaulisms in full bloom, and which we shall now consider in more detail.

Each nation associates a host of miscellaneous vulgarities, vices, diseases and disagreeable traits with foreign countries. The Japanese call foreigners "stinking of foreign hair" (*keto kusai*); the Czechs call a Hungarian a pimple (*uher*). In Hungary and Austria the cockroach is known as a Swabian (*swab, Schwabe*), in Poland as a Prussian (*prusak*) and in Germany as a Frenchman (*Franzose*). The French retaliate obliquely by calling the scurvy louse a Spaniard (*espagnol*). The Romans, however, with fine partiality named this troublesome insect after the Germans and the Poles, *latta germanica* and *coccus polonicus*. In Italy a privy has at times been known as an Englishman (*l'inglese*) and in Poland as a *Bismarck*, in honor of the Iron Chancellor. In England an errand to the privy has in former times been variously described as "to go to Egypt," "to take an Irish shave" or with the quaint euphemism "to give a Chinaman a music lesson." A malignant scalp ailment is commonly known as the Polish disease, the rickets as the English disease. Syphilis, originally the name of a shepherd in a Latin poem published in 1530, was called the Corinthian disease by the Greeks, the Spanish gout by the English, the French disease by the Germans and the Florentine or Neapolitan disease by the French. One infected by this dread affliction was said by the Dutch "to have seen Spain" and by the French "to have gone to Sweden or to Bavaria" (*aller en Suède, aller en Bavière*—a playful allusion to the sweat cure: Fr. *suer*, *baver*, to sweat). The unnatural vice of buggery is associated with the heretical Bulgarians who were reputed by their orthodox adversaries to be steeped in this vile practice. The heretics were opposed to marriage and procreation as sinful but not to coitus as such, and hence did not discourage promiscuous relations and homosexuality. This movement, which the Church regarded as the heresy par excellence, was at its height at about A.D. 1000 in Bulgaria, whose inhabitants did not find the imputed vice altogether disagreeable. All heretics in time came to be called Bulgarians, Bulgari, Boulgres, Bugari, Bougres, *bougre* and finally our *bugger* which, by a common quirk in the history of morals, has in American speech lost it flagitious implications and become a term of affection.

Unlovely epithets, to continue this morbid theme, have been bandied about with a profligate hand. A cheat or sharper at cards is a "Greek" to the English and French and a loudmouth to the Arabs; the Dutch attribute excessive boasting to the French, the Portuguese to the Spanish and the English to the Gascons (gasconade); the Germans say "proud as a Spaniard" (*stolz wie ein Spanier*), the French "proud as a Scot" (*fier comme un Ecossais*) and the Rumanians "stubborn as a Bulgarian" (*încâpatănat ca un bulgar*). We take "French leave" but the French "English leave" (*filer a l'anglaise*); when Poles formerly took "German leave" (*abszd niemiecki*) they went bankrupt, which in French was "to go to Belgium" (*filer en Belgique*). To play a dirty trick is in French "to play a Chinese trick" (*faire une chinoiserie*), in Spanish "a Basque trick" (*basquerie*), in Polish "to pull a Swabian" (*oszwabic*), and in Yiddish "to repay in Turkish" (*abtun uf terkish*). Excessive drinking in Dutch is "to drink like a Pole" (Fr. *gris comme un Polonais*) and in Czech "to drink like a Dutchman"; to get drunk in Spanish is "to catch a Turk" (*coger una turca*). In Spanish "to be surrounded by Englishmen" means to be dunned by many creditors, and "to work for the English" is to work for nothing. The German "to do a Polish" refers to the practice of blowing the nose in one's hand.

Sarcastic references to other nationalities are common: German humor in Rumanian is a lack of humor (*humor nemţesc*), a German joke in Spanish means stale wit (*chiste alemán*) and in German a *Kalauer* is a poor pun, which is perhaps from the Fr. *calembour* plus an indirect reference to the town of Calau in Brandenburg. A petty quarrel over nothing is in French a German quarrel (*querelle d'Allemand*); inefficient management is in German Polish economy (*polnische Wirtschaft*); inept diplomacy in Rumanian is Bulgarian diplomacy (*diplomatie bulgareasca*) and empty threats are characterized by the proverb "Beware of the Bulgarian fleet and the Greek cavalry" (*Ferestete de flota bulgara si de cavaleria greceasca*). The Germans maliciously refer to the thumb as the Jewish index finger, to the inside pocket of one's coat as the Jewish mailbox and describe arrogant boastfulness, *per antiphrasin*, as "the combination of Prussian charm and Jewish modesty." The funny bone is in French *le petit Juif*. The Lat. *Teutonici sunt nati venerunt de culo Pilati* (The Teutons were born coming out of Pilate's fundament) is perhaps the unkindest cut of all.

Hardly a country, however small, has been spared. Crete has given us liars, Philistia snobs, Lesbos lesbians, Corinthia whoremongers, Cyprus prostitutes, the Italian city of Cerreto charlatans, the Aztecs shrimps (Fr. *aztèque*, a shrimp of a man). In Polish a loose woman is known as *fladra* (flounder) with a sly reference to the early female settlers from Flanders; an arab is in English a street urchin and in French a usurer. A "Swiss" is in Russian a doorman, in French a miser (*Point d'argent, point de Suisse*, no tickie, no shirtie). A Scotch marriage is a runaway marriage, a Scotch prize worse than no prize at all, and a Scotch fiddle is an itch; Scotch attorney is simply the name of a plant. *Irish*, used as an adjective, usually refers to poverty and the snobbery that often goes with it: Irish apricots are potatoes, Irish draperies cobwebs, Irish diamonds rock crystals and Irish luck undeserved good fortune. The Turks gave us a cock, honey, rugs, a bath and a towel and yet *Turk* is an opprobrious epithet: a robber in Persian, a liar in Spanish, a scapegoat in French (*tête de Turc*), a tyrant in English and a madman in Danish. The English verb *to turkish* means to bowdlerize a story or turn it into a fable. A Turkish medal is an undone button on the fly of one's trousers (which, as Uncle Toby recommends, should be closed except in time of war, like the temple of Janus), and the Fr. *installation à la turque* refers to a seatless privy. The small country of Wales has given us the choicest mutton and the best flannel, both derived from the delicate breed of sheep which roam the Welsh hills, and has contributed to the comforts of modern life the Welsh rabbit (rarebit?), that is, melted cheese spread on toasted bread and eaten by the poor as a substitute for rabbit. Yet, malice has been injected into the adjective *Welsh:* a Welsh ambassador is a cuckoo or smart Alec, a Welsh mile is a long and tedious mile, a Welsh pearl is a counterfeit pearl and a Welsh uncle no uncle at all but the first cousin of a parent. The verb *to welsh,* to do someone out of money which has been placed as a bet, is an opprobrious generalization.

The people singled out for special invective in ancient times were the Boeotians, whose boorish habits furnished the comic poets of Greece with many malicious comparisons, the best known of which is the pithy bucolic metaphor *Boeotian swine* which in time gained the immortality of a proverb. It has been urged in modification of this harsh comparison that the moral character of the swine was more leniently appraised by the ancients than it is today. Such an ill-natured epithet, however, could at no time have been flattering. To this day we speak of Boeotian boors, full-paunched Boeotians, Boeotian simplicity, Boeotian heads, ears, and so on. It is often met with in the works of Unamuno as an epithet of disdain. The hard sayings that have been circulated about that ancient people have all been collected in a sympathetic book on the subject by Rhys Roberts. It is an interesting commentary on human vanity that the Boeotians themselves seemed to have been unaware of the disdain in which the Athenians held them and, vilified as they were, affected a similar superiority by assigning odious epithets to other cities in their own province and spoke of the envy of Tanagra, the stupidity of Haliartus, the insolence of Thebes, the meddlesomeness of Coronea, the pretentiousness of Plataea and the contentiousness of Thespiae.

The stigma which in ancient times adhered to the Boeotians has in our day fallen to the lot of the Dutch, the Boeotians being sometimes alluded to anachronously as "the Dutchmen of Greece." The comparison is no doubt due to an excessive devotion to the pleasures of the table and the intemperate drinking habits which have been attributed to both nations. The ensuing sluggishness of mind and body induced by these habits is aggravated by the mephitic vapors which the inhabitants of both countries are compelled to breathe throughout the year. The additional circumstance that Holland was Britain's chief economic rival in the seventeenth century did not help to endear her to the English, for whom she was "the off-scouring of the British sand and the undigested vomit of the sea." This accounts for the prolific derisiveness embodied in the adjective *Dutch* in our language: a Dutch auction opens with a high bid and gradually works down, a Dutch bargain is a one-sided bargain generally concluded at the drinking table, a Dutch steak is a hamburger, a Dutch reckoning a disputed bill, a Dutch nightingale a frog, a Dutch widow a strumpet, a Dutch wife a poor bed companion; "my old Dutch" refers to one's wife whose face resembles an old Dutch clock; Dutch courage is induced by drink (*bravoure après boire*); a Dutch defense is an abject surrender; to talk like

67

a Dutch uncle is to give a paternal sermon; at a Dutch concert each singer stubbornly proceeds with his own tune and at a Dutch feast the host is drunk by the time the guests arrive. What we call "going Dutch" the French call "going English or Swiss" (*faire une anglaise, suisse*) and what the French call "German happiness" (*le bonheur allemand*) we call "Dutch comfort." The Dutch themselves have made no attempt to retaliate, contenting themselves with some stray allusions to the Scots as unmannerly louts and they call a dirty trick a German trick (*moffenstreik*). This enviable absence of rancor is typical of the forbearing spirit of the land that gave birth to such champions of tolerance as Grotius, Erasmus and Spinoza, every whit as noble as Hesiod, Pindar and Plutarch, who saw the light amid the heavy mists of Boeotia. Voltaire's parting shot on leaving Holland, "Adieu, cannaux, canards, canaille" (canals, ducks, rabble), owes more to his irresistible urge for alliteration than to malice.

These gloomy reflections have perhaps been carried far enough. It suffices to indicate a natural propensity of intolerance rooted in our national life, and ultimately in a melancholy imperfection in our personal outlook. We naturally mistrust a stranger who does not speak our language, for we have no means of deciphering his unexpressed thoughts and hence have no access to his mind:

> The stranger within our gate
> He may be true and kind
> But he does not talk my talk—
> I cannot feel his mind.
> I see the face and the eyes and the mouth
> But not the soul behind.

X *Adam Bows Low*

According to the theory of the last chapter we have access to another mind only through some kind of intellectual reconstruction by means of audible verbal symbols. Language is the only means by which we can interpret another's mind and relive another's emotions. However, the world is loath to yield its secrets to the human ear. Sound, to use a mischievous homonym, is an unsound plummet with which to sound the depths of life. The human ear is not always attuned to catch the muffled word. The eye is better equipped to decipher the world, for a reflection is truer than an echo: "Eyes are vocal, tears have tongues,/ And there be words not made by lungs." From this point of view human language is derived from graphic representations of universally comprehensible gestures addressed to the eye. Thought can best be reconstructed from actions. Access to other minds is gained by observing behavior and thus entering immediately, not inferentially, into alien emotions. According to a Chinese legend language was first brought to man in the form of signs written on a turtle's back. Not the audible sounds from the turtle's mouth but the markings on its carapace were to serve man as the touchstone to decode nature's secrets. This is the basis of the gesture theory of language or what we may call the

"quack-quack theory," which can be illustrated by the gestures
made by foreigners when ordering a meal in a strange country:

Moo: I cried for milk—
If I wanted bread
My jaws I set agoing,
And asked for new-laid eggs
By clapping hands and crowing.

Instinctively aware of this modern insight, Adam preceded his
verbal introduction discussed in the last chapter with a low bow.
We are here in the presence of a phenomenon, now on the decline, which owes its operation not to a snobbish or merely
esthetic impulse but to an instinctive gesture built into the structure of the body. The criticism of democratic derogators that
Adam abandoned the upright position natural to man's dignity
to adopt a feudal posture of defenselessness is not well taken.
Adam's temporary departure from the perpendicular is not to be
construed as a lapse from rectitude. It bore no signs of effete
prudery or impaired vitality. On the contrary, this apparently
superfluous gesture, accompanied by several handsprings and
capers, was a therapeutic improvisation calculated to work off
Adam's satyriasis and restore the blood to his head. At the same
time it served as a *ruse de guerre* to show off his figure with a
view to seduction, consisting of funambulating saltations which
Darwin recommends to the courting male (for what female can
resist a dancing lover!) and including, according to the
Freudians, a prurient examination of the genitals. These antics
required a degree of agility seldom seen today. Modern man
is phlegmatic in courtship, which he conducts in a sitting position on the lounge or in a parked vehicle in order to save his
legs, with a solemn expression on his face and often with his
hands in his pockets. While immersed in these acrobatics, Adam
bellowed forth in song ("I was made for you and you were

70

made for me"), falling head over heels (originally, heels over head) for the object of his serenade. Even then it was required of a lover to spend some time at his beloved's feet before he fell into her hands. For a woman requires more than stolen glances, apprehensive sighs or the *parola ornata* of asteism (urbane wit) as tangible proof of man's devotion.

The scholarly approach is deadly to love. Women are not attracted by siren notes as are frogs, by the amorous touch as salamanders, by brilliant colors as the Siamese fighting fish or by odiferous secretions to which the she-goat succumbs. Woman needs a dramatic act to create an atmosphere for love, a bold gesture of magnanimity in which the male risks life and limb in her behalf. Adam's bow was such a gesture. To bow low to the ground whence he came was to expose his most vulnerable organ to a fellow human being, a highly specialized part of the body which contains a delicate brain encased in hard bone and having on its frontal part all the chief organs of sense, except that of touch. In the animal kingdom the assumption of a defenseless position in the face of an enemy elicits an instinctive withdrawal of the attacker. A defenseless animal can awaken compassion by exposing an unprotected part to its assailant who thereupon chivalrously desists, unable to attack. No such provision has been made in human beings, for whom an appeal for mercy may go unheeded. Altruism is not implanted in man but is fostered by education and social restraints. It was, therefore, an unprecedented act of faith in that experimental period of human history for Adam to lower his head in salutation.

In this boisterous dance approach astute critics like Havelock Ellis, Karl Bühler and Otto Jespersen profess to see the origin of work rhythms, religious rituals, the ballet and language itself. To the hi-de-ho theory they add the yo-heave-ho theory. This theory, which explains Adam's bow as that of a timid animal in an effort to overcome his reticence, overlooks the spiritual as-

71

pects of that generous gesture. An explanation more in keeping with first man's epic life is that the bow was a dumb gesture of chivalry performed as an act of pure faith. Chivalry gives an exalted status to woman because she is weaker (except when in league with the Devil) and imposes upon the man social forms of deference, such as tactful words, polite formulas and obsequious gestures. Some of these forms of salutation are painful and incommodious, as taking off shoes, rubbing noses, cracking fingers or exposing one's head, however bald, in inclement weather on greeting a lady outdoors. A more agreeable manner of conventional greeting is the kiss which is given by way of salutation or as a sign of subservience. The kiss was formerly more widespread. Latin has three words for kiss: *osculum* (confined to the cheek), *basium* (implanted on the lips) and *suavium* (reserved for lovers). The kiss of humility has disappeared, except for the kiss of the Pope's toe; and the ceremonial kiss is common only among the French. The Austrians and the Hungarians still kiss the hands of ladies and use *Küss die Hand* as a greeting for both sexes. Spain, however, where the kiss has fled and left only the empty form: *Póngame Ud. a los pies q.b. de su señora* (Give my regards to your wife, or, literally, Put me at the feet, which I kiss, of your wife) abbreviates the words *que beso*, which I kiss, and places them before the genitive to indicate that it is the feet and not the lady herself that are being kissed. The Spanish *besalamano* refers to a brief communication to another person, usually written on a visiting card, as: "Antonio Caso b.l.m. al Sr. Don Pedro y le ruega . . ." Antonio Caso kisses the hand of Sr. Don Pedro and requests him . . ." The word *besalamano* has gone over into French (*baselementer*, to kiss the hand), into German dialect (*Bezelmanos*, flatterer) and into Danish (*Basleman*).

The gesture theory regards language as primarily visual, and seeks its origin in the hand, the mouth and in the joints of the body. The pantomime of the body furnishes the vital impulse reflected in the written word which is at bottom the embodiment of a gesture and bears the imprint of its spatial and motor origin. Words have definite shapes, textures and hues which the poet can weave into curious patterns. For the eye of a poet sees a definite relation between the looks of a word and its meaning. The word *happy* looks more carefree than *gay*, and *grey* is a shade greyer than *gray* because the *a* admits more light than the *e*. In the Italian word for man, *omo*, Dante fancied he saw the human face itself, the two *o*'s standing for the eyes and the *m* for the nose and cheekbones. The preoccupation with the physical form of a word goes back to the Stoic theory of analogy which held that there is an intimate relation between the appearance of a word and its meaning. The *length* of a word, for example, should be commensurate with the thing it signifies. Under the influence of this theory Lucilius made his nominative plurals longer than the singular. Aquila, who made a literal translation of the Bible into Greek, went to great lengths to preserve the corresponding size of the words. For example, he rendered Heb. *yaḥdov* with Gr. *homou*, since both words contain the same number of letters, begin and end with a vowel, and so on—a dextrous piece of verbal carpentry which must have required a firm hand and an iron will. We are still conscious of the size of words. Shaw complained that *love* was too small a word for so big a thing. A large fish in Hawaii is called *ô* and a very small fish is known by the lingual leviathan *homomomonukunukuaguk*. The name of Lloyd George's birthplace, a small town in Wales, is Llanfairpwllgwyngyllgogergchwyrndrobwillandisiliogogogoch.

The problem of a word's physiognomy assumes great importance in exegesis, where the slightest change in a letter is fraught with far-reaching consequences. The translators of the Greek version of the Bible, known as the Septuagint or LXX, were confronted with the problem of finding a Greek equivalent for the Tetragrammaton, the ineffable four-letter name of God, a name which would reflect the original graphic form in which its mystic charm was believed to reside. A profane transcription of the Name was precluded since Greek-speaking Jews, for whom the translation was intended, were forbidden to utter the sacred Name even in its Greek form. The translators were faced with two possibilities: either to leave the Name in its original form and retain the mystery (adopted by Aquila in his literal translation which is preserved in Origen's *Hexapla*) or render it by a Greek word whose written form would not reveal its exact meaning. The two words finally chosen were *kyrios* for Adonai, the traditional substitute pronunciation for Yahwe, and *theos* for Elohim. These names were not written out but contracted to K̄C̄ and Θ̄C̄, with the horizontal virgula placed by Greeks above foreign names, proper nouns and transliterated words. Luther was faced with the same problem centuries later and ingeniously resolved the difficulty (which he discusses in the introduction to his Old Testament translation) by a visual distinction, rendering Yahwe as *heRR* and Adonai as *HErr*.

The eye as well as the ear has imagination and takes delight in visual effects. Religious writers have always cultivated visual alliteration for mystical reasons. Among the Greeks, Hipponax of Ephesus, a satiric poet of the fifth century B.C., called *The Pungent* because of his biting satire, violated the rhythmical structure of his poems by maliciously ending his iambics with a spondee or trochee. These lame or crabbed verses, known as choliambi, were designed to reflect the perversity of human nature and are in poetry what a cripple is in nature. Whole poems have been constructed for the eye by a technique called technopaegnia. The inventor of this form is said to have been the Greek poet Theodoric, who composed poems shaped like axes, gloves, bottles, eggs and frying pans. Illustrations of this literary mannerism are also to be found among the poets of the Metaphysical School. It has been said of Gautier's poems that all they needed was a frame and a hook. Victor Hugo expressed the view that words are primarily to be looked at and not to be read aloud, and hence he fell into the habit of staring intently at the written page while composing. Poets often intend rhymes for the eye alone. Thus, Wordsworth rhymes *one* with *stone* and Tennyson *sword* with *word;* in the humorous verse of Ogden Nash we find *golf* rhymed with *wolf,* and *wed* with *Wed.* Eye rhymes abound in French poetry, where masculine rhymes ending with a consonant or a sounded vowel alternate with feminine rhymes ending with a mute *e,* the appeal being to the eye alone because there is no difference, for example, in the sound of the homonyms *mer* and *mère.* Hence *Vénus* is an acceptable rhyme for *venus,* the endings serving only as mute ornaments to satisfy the French sense for visual symmetry, and resounding in the mind alone. On the other hand, where the English may rhyme *bay* with *weigh* the French may not rhyme *raison* with *saisons* or *mort* with *remords,* for these words do not agree in spelling and their dissimilar contours offend the French eye.

The visual impact of words has lost its appeal for modern man, who dismisses the whole subject as an idle amusement. He thinks of himself as the master of words who can mutilate them as he sees fit. Many words have been changed in the course of time through intent or ignorance and are none the worse for it: *scissors,* derived from *cysowres* and formerly written *cissors,* was changed to its present form by scholars deliberately to make it conform to Lat. *scissus.* English spelling is a monumental witness to the misguided erudition of pedants and printers. Words like *scythe, sieve, scent* and *rhyme* do not reflect their origin in their present appearance; and conversely, the same letter *o* is differently pronounced in *one, women, whose, clock, kimono* and *Lincoln.* English spelling does not reflect the spoken word, and could be abolished entirely in favor of shorthand without impairing communication. We are in reality spelling imaginary sounds. The appearance of a word is irrelevant: different meanings can be attached to the same word (*sound, mean, bill*); a word can be given a different meaning when differently pronounced (*sewer, wound, lead*); and the same significance may adhere to words which do not look alike. Examples of the latter are words transliterated from a foreign alphabet which, despite a difference in appearance, still retain their original sound and meaning, as in Origen's *Hexapla* in which the first two columns give the original Hebrew followed by its equivalent in Greek characters, or in Rashi's famous commentary to the Pentateuch which contains many French words in Hebrew script and is a valuable source for determining French pronunciation of the twelfth century, or Mendelssohn's German translation of the Psalms in Hebrew characters. This is also true in those cases where the alphabet of one language is used to render the sounds of another: Ladino, which writes Spanish in Hebrew characters, Persian which is written with Arabic characters, and so on. Two alphabets may be employed to render the sounds of the *same* language, as Urdu and Hindi, which employ the Arabic and Devanagari characters, respectively. Thus, a native of India may be able to converse with one from Pakistan and yet be unable to read the same newspaper; conversely, two Chinese who can read the same newspaper may find their audible speech mutually untelligible. Serious poets in lighter moments have concocted poems in which they utilize the same *sounds* of two different languages; as, S. D. Luzzato's composition beginning *Ah! l'uom misero è* . . . (Heb. *Hal'om mi ze roeh* . . .) which can be understood when read *aloud* by both an Italian and a Hebrew, although in different senses.

According to the "convention theory" the meaning of a word is determined by custom and usage and not by its facial expression or delicate design. For a window shopper to study the quality of the glass and pay no heed to the contents displayed in the window can only lead to spurious profundity. And yet no age has worshiped the sounds and forms of words more than ours, with a sensuous idolatry more grievous than that from which Abraham sought to preserve Israel. The body of a word is part and parcel of its meaning, the very lifeblood of the word itself—like the image of a stained church window on whose elaborate designs the pious gaze with reverence. We all have subjective preferences for the sounds of particular words, apart from their meanings. Coleridge was fond of *harberous*, Joyce of *smithereens*, Gautier of *blanc* and *cygne*, and the German word *Geige*, violin, was to Leibniz's ear a true rendering of the tone of that instrument; Thomas Hood hated the very sound of *charity*, De Quincey detested the word *quibbling* and on George Eliot's lips the word *crudity* stood for all that was distasteful and objectionable. Some prefer pompous words like *illecebrous, sphacelate, pruriginous* or *ichoglan*. I myself, however, am fond of simple words like *swink, pheeze, thole, ickle, sneb* and perhaps *clogdogdo* and am repelled by such bloated words as *efficiency, integration, organize, financial* and all words relating to money (except *baldmoney*, which is another name for the umbelliferous spicknel, and *dollardee*, which is the name for the bluegill).

That the appearance of a word *is* important calls to mind an amusing story, accompanied by an appropriate illustration, found in Thomas Hood's *Collected Works*, concerning an Englishman who, while touring the East, found himself in a sedan rickshaw with neither top nor bottom but with only two sides between which he ran on foot, a circumstance which induced him to remark that he might indeed just as well have walked, *"except for the looks of the thing."*

 XI *Cavilers, Borborites and Zoilists*

Adam, more than any other man, lends himself to abuse. He has evoked the strongest antipathy among the theologians who portray his regrettable lapse in alarming colors. While he lived in Eden, they fawned on him. But when he fell and lay groveling in the dust, rundown and half crushed, these rhyparographers (portrayers of low life) detect eccentricities and shortcomings, however far fetched, in order to deride him. It is easy to dwell on the faults of departed greatness, especially of such a controversial figure as first man. We shall not defend Adam's imperfections or singularities nor hush the scandal which arose from his first disobedience. But we shall take the scourge from the hands of these indiscriminate critics and deflate the triumphant language in which they exult.

Adam's uninspired critics fall into three classes: cavilers, borborites and zoilists. Cavilers (OF *caviller*, to mock or rail) are fault finders who become entangled in subtleties while looking for loopholes and are not to be confused with *cavaliers*. Borborites (Gr. *bórboros*, filth) are those who hold filthy or immoral doctrines and indulge in borborology or obscene talk. The word is not related to *borborygm*, which is a rumbling in the bowels, a serious annoyance more common than the word. A zoilist (from Zoilus, a Greek cynic of the fourth century B.C., noted for his bitter attacks on Homer and Plato) refers to a censorious and envious critic and is not to be confused with a Zolaist, a follower of the French novelist Zola. All three are interested in maligning Adam: the first by inveighing against his character, the second by detracting from his physical perfection and the third by belittling his linguistic accomplishments.

The cavilers never tire of pointing out that the Tree of Life in the Garden was in reality a vine, for all evil flows from alcohol. Adam sinned while drunk on wine. Etymological support for this opinion is found in the Hebrew word for wine, *yayin*, which is the sound both of wine and of wailing. This view is not as harsh as that which takes the Tree of Life to be a phallus, based on the text in Proverbs: "It is a Tree of Life; happy is he who lays hold of it." Wine, however, has always been regarded as a healthful stimulant, cheering God and man, and metaphorically as representing the essence of all goodness. The cavilers affect the tongue of virtue but are obviously intent on establishing the *fons et origo* of human history in a crapulent Forefather. They would do better to ponder the more pious interpretation revealed in Scripture: "A wholesome tongue is the Tree of Life" (Proverbs 15:4). Similarly, one caviler pretends to doubt that Adam was a vegetarian in order to cast aspersion on his gentle nature, for meat eaters are troubled with strong sensual desires. This invidious reflection, however, is the result of ignorance and is without Scriptural support. Adam was given dominion over the beasts of the field only for purposes of exploiting their labor (Genesis 1:28), not for butchery. Adam lived on a strict herbaceous diet of fruit, lettuce and greens on which he thrived as did Daniel after him (Daniel 1:5–16). It is a matter of common knowledge that Noah was the first meat eater when the distressing conditions on the

79

Ark compelled him to eat flesh in order to sustain his diminishing bodily vigor. It was then that he acquired a taste for mastodon steaks, dinosaur cuts, fried ichthyosaurus and such delicacies as sow's udders, roasted ants and tender leopard's womb (cooked, of course). In time man became the most omnivorous of all scavengers, requiring at least one meat meal a day, usually in the evening (Numbers 11:31–34). The term *vegetarianism* is a vague one and comprises a bewildering variety of prohibitions—fish, eggs, the wearing of leather shoes, and so on—depending on the ethical, practical or esthetic motives which prompt its adherents. But even in the strictest view Adam was a vegetarian to his very marrow. There is no room here for dispute.

We now come to a consideration of two borborite arguments more difficult to dispose of, both concerned with first man's physical imperfection. The first is the disturbing question put to theologians to state whether Adam was furnished with a navel. For if he had one it was superfluous; and if he did not it was an oversight—in either case an imperfection. This is a knotty problem, which the author has not investigated and on which he is loath to hazard an opinion. Fortunately, the subject is not touched in the case of Eve, whose "tortuous and complicated nodosity" reverent artists have thoughtfully covered with long, yellow hair. The second borborite detraction takes us even further afield into the malicious inquiry of Adam's circumcision. If the sign of the covenant was not cut in his flesh, it was a serious blemish. For circumcision is not a mere tribal mark, like a tattoo or the knocking out of front teeth or a hygienic measure to prevent phimosis, but a sign of perfection and a mark of nobility. Since the covenant was inaugurated much later with Abraham, the problem becomes complicated. But not insuperable! Rabbi Judah answers the malevolent critic by affirming that Adam was created circumcised but later stooped to practice epispasm; that is, he removed the sign of circumcision. The rabbi

80

deduced this unedifying act from the verse in Hosea: "Like Adam they have transgressed the covenant." There is no point in carrying this inquiry further except to repeat the words of the prophet that true circumcision is that of the heart (Jeremiah 4:14).

The borborite attempt, later continued by the naturalists, to show that man is faultily constructed is not in accord with the traditional account. The Lord lavished great care on His *chef-d'oeuvre*. He first took counsel with the angels and then made a rough draft or *golem* which He proceeded to elaborate with the detail that properly belongs to a work of love. The angels then kneaded him and when they finished they bowed down to him, except Satan. Originally, man was created androgynous, with two faces, a tail and a scaly skin which, except for the fingernails, fell off after the Fall. To form Adam the Lord had gathered the dust from all parts of the earth: the trunk from Babylon, the head from Palestine and the private parts from Akra de Agma, a town near Pumbeditha which was notorious for the loose morals of its inhabitants. His eye alone was the image of the world: his eyeball the earth, the white of the eye the encircling oceans, the iris the dry land, the pupil the Temple of Jerusalem. In short, Adam was a macrocosm:

> When God at first made Man,
> Having a glass of blessings standing by;
> Let us (said He) pour on him all we can:
> Let the world's riches, which dispersèd lie,
> Contract into a span.
>> —George Herbert,
>> "The Gifts of God"

Man was made to be master of nature: the sea divided before Moses, the sun stood still before Joshua, the ravens fed Elijah, the lions refused to devour Daniel, the whale spewed up Jonah and the heavens opened to Ezekiel. No wonder Adam was pleased

81

with the many excellencies conferred upon his person and in gratitude shook Eden's air with a lyrical verse from the Psalms: "I am fearfully and wonderfully made; how great are Thy works, O Lord." Here we see clearly that the first fruits of human speech were not the zoological names Adam gave the beasts but a paean in praise of Him who created man. On the wings of this verse man wafted back to God his homage and "rendered back to Heaven in praise harmonious the first air he drew." It is disconcerting to note, however, that in true romantic fashion man admired himself first and *then* praised his Creator.

Finally, the zoilists' criticism revolves around Adam's linguistic ability and is thus closer to our theme. Their strictures are directed against his faulty spelling, his limited vocabulary and his defective comprehension. The first animadversion, made by a pasquinader whose name has been mercifully withheld, takes the form of an innocent question of orthography; namely, Did Adam put the hyphen in jackass? If the traducer is referring to the long-eared beast that brays uproariously, the answer is that Adam did insert the hyphen since the novelty of the combination was still fresh in his mind: *jack* was a separate word referring to the male of a species, usually half-sized, and prefixed to a number of different kinds of creatures—the jack-crow bird, the jack-salmon fish and the jackass-rabbit, so-called because of its long ears. *He-ass* retains the hyphen for phonetic reasons and the plural form *jack-asses* for esthetic reasons; the nonce words *to jackass, jackassery* and *jackassification* are unhyphenated, although *jackass-driver* is written with a hyphen and *jackass critic* treated as two separate words for obvious reasons. To argue the matter further is, in the words of an old Greek proverb, "to contend for the shadow of a jackass." It is regrettable that we have no word in our language comparable to that most useful Spanish verb *desasnar*, to "unass" a dolt who asks silly questions and teach him refinement. The truth of the matter is that Adam not only put the hyphen in *jack-ass* to distinguish man from beast (*Jack, ass*) but, what is more significant, omitted it from *theology* (*theos, logos*) to bridge the gap between God and man and relate the loosely knit empirical world of blind chance and brute accident to the world of the spirit. Human speech now acquired meaning by establishing its fundamental allegiance in the Infinite, its root and anchor. With this alliance Adam brought heaven and earth together and like Hamlet could say, "I could be bounded in a nutshell and count myself a king of infinite space."

The stricture against Adam's limited vocabulary is made by a zoilist with a more scientific turn of mind who is unduly disturbed by the absence of the fish during the Great Review and demands to know why these cold-blooded creatures were not present when the animals marked time and the birds stopped in midair to be christened by first man. Milton, in his grand epic, condescends to answer this carping critic by pointing out that Eden was inland and that the fish could not have been summoned from their watery residence and "change their element to draw the thinner air." This reason, though elegantly expressed, holds no water, for many fish are known to be at home on terra firma. There is no truth in the ditty that "the fish when he's exposed to air, displays no trace of *savoir faire*." Flying fish undertake short journeys through the air, perch climb trees, and crabs make nuptial pilgrimages to the coast. Adam did not name the fish because he was not commissioned to do so. Had the fish reported to him on Naming-Day they would not have received such ugly ichthyic names as *mudskipper, fish-hog,* such obscure appellations as *herring, haddock, shark,* or such corruptions as *lobster* (Lat. *locusta*) and *halibut* (*holy butt,* because it is eaten on holy days).

The strongest disparagement, however, is directed against Adam's defective understanding and comes from our own Mark Twain. In his opinion Adam had been punished too severely for his "nursery trespass." Adam was hungry for an apple, and hunger knows no principles. In a satirical mood Mark Twain pictures the Father of Mankind as a good-natured nincompoop who was unable to cope with the ontological novelties before him. When he first beheld Cain, he mistook the infant for a kangaroo and was about to take it apart and stuff it for his collection when Eve intervened. As a linguist Adam cut a poor figure, unable to tell a P-cock from a Q-cumber, an ant from a pheasant, a puss from an octopus or an antelope from a cantaloupe. It was Eve who prompted him when he bungled the names of the animals, and thus saved the day. Dante, who had studied this phase of Adam's career more sympathetically, does not share our cynical author's unrestrained admiration for Eve. He finds it unseemly that so exalted an act of the human race as speech should first proceed from woman. He therefore chides Eve for usurping Adam's function and presuming to speak first. This is a manly opinion and is to be put down to the poet's admiration for the Alpha of the Race, "our ancient Sire, to whom every bride is both daughter and daughter-in-law." The ancient Brahmans, on the other hand, did not find it unreasonable to believe that a woman should have been the first to speak, and hence did not shrink from attributing the invention of language to Sarasvati, the wife of Brahma. Here we have two schools of male psychology (or mythology) with respect to women: woman as inspiration and woman as impediment, the first being associated with the Anglo-Saxon and the second with the Latin tradition. Manu, the Hindu Noah who was warned by the fish to build an ark, took no female into the boat but trusted to the ingenuity of the gods to preserve the race.

These melancholy expressions of disparagement are, for the most part, animated by a gnostic inclination to derogate Adam's endowments and to magnify his peccadilloes. Adam's failure to name the flowers, however, is not to be confused with these irreverent squibs. This was a serious omission due to more than an oversight. These bright jewels, God's first creation when He planted the Garden, grew at his very feet and filled the air with fragrance. Did he find it too incommodious to stoop and scrutinize these floral edifices and give them some adorable name? Were they too lowly to engage his languid interest bent on more practical affairs? The mind that found clear-cut nouns for the animals was too prosaic to invent names for these whimsical gems "of His unrivalled pencil"—Aaron's beard, Dutchman's breeches, blue-eyed Mary, jack-in-the-pulpit and kiss-me-at-the-garden-gate, or devise sobriquets for the darling daisy, the coquettish pansy, the impatient touch-me-not, the elecampane moist with Helen's tears, the hyacinth streaked with Spartan blood and the ravishing catmint which transports cats into fits of catniption. Adam failed to recognize even those flowers which should have been familiar to him—the horsetail, the goosefoot, the larkspur (which resembles the hind claw of the lark), the geranium (shaped like the crane's bill, Gr. *geranos*, crane), the ranunculaceous buttercup (diminutive of Lat. *rana*, little frog), and even Adam's-needle, the state flower of New Mexico. Adam's diffidence may have stemmed from his envy of the flowers' supernatural adaptation, their independence of animal life, their quiet absorption of dew and air, their sexless reproduction and their freedom from original sin. Or he may have detected in the narcotic daffodil, the poisonous hemlock and the baneful locoweed ominous portents of man's transient estate and a foreboding of the fate soon to overtake him.

Adam refrained from naming the flowers because his esthetic sensibilities were still undeveloped. His geometric mind was not at home in a world of adjectives, his heart was not yet aglow with esthetic radiance: a primrose by the river's side was just a primrose to him. He was not yet on friendly terms with the world, the flesh and the devil. Until Eve came along! She entered this flowery reserve hedged about with incantatory signs, allured by color and odor. She appreciated the perfumed songs and amatory brightnesses of these matchless treasures, and they in turn saluted her as a sister flower and begged to be crushed under her foot that they might exude their rich odors:

> Eve, fleur de ma vie, o ma femme, o
> Salut, fleur de beauté, ma soeur!
> Et que si ton pied nous écrase
> Nous ressentons come une extase
> De volupté.

It must be urged in Adam's defense that flowers were not an integral part of his scheme of things at this early stage in his career. At most they formed a colorful backdrop for the Animal Parade and the drama of human life. Not that he was too haughty to gather wisdom from them or too busy to watch them grow! But he would not enfeeble his solid mind by peering for wisdom in the crannied wall. He hankered after universal categories in the luminous realm of the spirit. The pursuit of truth and the practical ends of morality engrossed his soul.

XII *The First Oath and the Crowing of the Cock*

About two hours after the Naming Review our First Parents were driven from their home. A clap of thunder burst upon them while they were still having lunch alfresco. The jig was up. Before they knew it they found themselves with Eden behind them and a gloomy wilderness before them. Without a shirt on their backs, so to speak, they were cast adrift, for better or worse, in an unfriendly world which, like every man after them, they had to fashion anew. For a brief moment our Parents lingered in the gray twilight of two worlds, between a *No More* and a *Not Yet*. Then the outcasts took hasty farewell of their birthplace, burning through Eden's branches, and, casting a regretful look eastward, made their exit into a fearful world of sorrow—in the ambiguous words of an indignant English writer: "Adam hurried with his blooming wife out of their blasted Paradise."

Since prudence was not a virtue which distinguished our Parents, they had made no provision for the misfortune which overtook them. As night closed in on them, the dispossessed couple sought refuge in the forgetfulness of slumber. This was their first sleep and last rest. Sleep, which brings balm to sorrow, must have been an exquisite pleasure for these transgressors. What monstrous thoughts racked their aboriginal minds as they lay amid the thorns and thistles of the gloomy vale outside Eden! Were their primal brains convulsed by the precipitate Fall and its ensuing penalties? Could they have foreseen that the present state of their minds would become the battleground of future controversy concerning the nature of human depravity, a controversy which would divide men forever into Augustinians and Pelagianists? Little did they dream that the naming of the animals that morning, meagerly recorded in the two verses of the biblical text, would give rise to a voluminous literature (including the present volume) which goes under the name of "lingua adamaica," given to it by the German mystic Jakob Böhme! A plausible rabbinic legend informs us that the evening of the Fall fell on the New Year, the traditional Day of Judgment. This was a fortunate circumstance for all concerned. It permits our disreputable Parents to reflect on the nature of their moral declension and the bitter fruits of rebellion while we, their progeny, who are still discharging the penalties of their transgression, are left to speculate on the woes that the Fall brought to mankind and on the insoluble linguistic problems which, among others, it bequeathed to us.

On the following morning Eve was awakened by her spouse. This was a rude awakening. She would have preferred to sleep and not face the morning light, for she felt guilty and sullen. Their roles had now been reversed: in Eden she had awakened him, that is, she had opened his eyes by giving him the apple; in Exile he was to be the Awakener of sleeping nature, the eternal Promethean rebel. They now rose from their thorny couch in a lamentable condition. A day begun in rapture had ended in agony. They were still rankling from their recent injury. On their drowsy eyes were the signs of a night spent in conjugal passion, for the motion of concupiscence was, according to St. Augustine, the first consequence of the Fall and a direct sequel of the first sin. The lusting flesh, demanding gratification, was in rebellion against man's rational faculties. In Eden, Adam had been free from the assaults of the flesh. But the eating of the aphrodisiac apple had now wrought disorders in his body, and removed the sex organs from his conscious control. Conjugation was now a matter of frenzied urgency, entailing more pain than pleasure. The first offspring of this fallen procreation was a murderer.

At this point Adam's attention was diverted to a loftier organ of his body. While putting on his shoes (which he had great difficulty in buttoning) he felt a tickling in the gallery of his nostrils, induced by the strong-scented sneezewort, whereupon, without the consent of his will, he trumpeted forth an ejection of vapor from his head in the form of a sneeze, which sounded to his ears somewhat like *hupshi* or *whoseshe*. Adam had sneezed only once before, when God breathed the breath of life into him, on which occasion he uttered, according to the Koran, the blessing, "Al-hamdu Allah." From then until the time of Jacob, a man would sneeze once and then die, a curious swan song. But now God did not carry out His threat to take Adam's life and, finding himself still alive, Adam recited the prescribed prophylactic verse, "I have waited for Thy salvation, O Lord" (Genesis 49:18). Adam should have taken St. Augustine's advice (*De Doctrina Christiana* ii.120) to return to bed as soon as he felt the ominous tickle. A sneeze defies explanation. It is not self-induced like eructations from the inferior parts for it is beyond conscious control. The itch demands immediate attention but it can be alleviated by a variety of methods, dictated by the constitution of the species: the bird uses its beak, the dog its hind paws, the horse (who cannot use his extremities) rubs the affected part against a tree or rolls on the ground, the elephant draws up water in his trunk and blows it down his back, the duck stands on one leg and scratches with the other. Man, however, is not dependent on any particular organ for scratching. He can use an external implement for those places he cannot reach with his hand or he can ask a fellow man to do the scratching. A sneeze, however, cannot be delegated. It is a temporary convulsion as uncontrollable as the procreative act to which, in folklore, it is related. The victim must wait in alarm and consternation until his physical frame has been jolted and the nasal storm has run its course.

It was on the heels of this significant incident that Adam, glaring at her whom he had until then complaisantly called his "better half," let loose an oath so tremendous that it startled the birds in midair and caused Eve to execute an involuntary movement. It was an imprecation so foul that, bachelor as I am, I shall refrain from repeating, except to say that it is an optative interjection with no subject expressed and taken by foreigners as a shibboleth of our tongue. The sounds of the oath may be found in the palindrome with which Adam had introduced himself to Eve the day before, wherein they constitute the second and the last syllables, for a blessing and a curse, though differing in intent, are often composed of the same sounds. It is the kind of oath to be expected from a sensitive man in a similar predicament. Adam had more right to utter an oath than Job or King Lear. He had been reduced to the worst poverty that fortune can lay upon human flesh. He had been visited with the severest calamity that can befall a man. The abrupt transition had unsettled him. He had to face the world single-handed, with feelings of guilt, the fear of death and all this impransus (without breakfast). Adam could not suppress an incredulous smile at the incongruence and absurdity of his predicament. But his smile was short-lived as he reflected on the damp prospects before him.

So deeply imbedded is this oath in human nature that many scholars profess to see in it the painful expression of frustrated sexual desire and the very root of human speech itself. The original vigorous motor and perceptual qualities of the oath are now difficult to detect behind the refined euphemisms and distortions which have rendered the intimate relation between sound and image more opaque and hence less objectionable. Many words with scatological connotations have gone underground: *donkey* and *rooster* have replaced *ass* and *cock* in recent versions of the Bible; the Navy has officially dropped *coxswain* from its vocabulary. Latin words ending in *pedo*, as *intercapedo*, interval, were avoided because the word *pedo* meant "flatulence," euphemistically defined by a saint in the Middle Ages as "a suppressed sigh." In his "Sunday Screw" Charles Dickens innocently defined a screw as "a little instrument remarkable for its curious twist," but it would take a bold man to hazard a public reading of this short tale today. Our squeamish age has resorted to phonetic distortion (*nerts* for *nuts*) and typographical devices such as asterisks, dashes (d——n, d————d, G—d). These castrated imprecations shield us from the imputation of impiety; the ear is satisfied while the eye retains its innocence.

Obscene expletives retain their original force longer than other words because (since they seldom sully our lips) they are not subjected to normal wear and tear. Many of them, being connected with the digestive and evacuative phases, come to us from the childhood of the race. Even in the midst of our refinement they well up instinctively from the interior part of our being, like the neigh of a horse or the grunt of swine. These are the non-linguistic forms of communication inherited by Adam from the animals. A sensitive ear can still discern them in the modern vernacular which has replenished its inherited store with new creations: *tail, fanny* and *fairy* have been put to new uses; *goose* and *neck* have assumed additional functions as verbs; *cock* plus *tail* have been made respectable by being combined; *bitch*, which has yielded in some circles to *lady-dog*, has made a comeback as a verb in the sense of "to complain" and as the abbreviation *s.o.b.* Where vocal expression is throttled, this urge takes the devious form of coprophemia (indecent gestures, wolf whistles, writing obscene words on walls, and so on).

Expletives and obscene oaths still invigorate our lethargic speech. Although divorced from language and denied the status of parts of speech, these words elicit from us a direct and instantaneous reaction. Bismarck, who was not regarded as a man of pronounced verbal delicacy, was moved to remark on one occasion when interrupted by an audible *Pfui* from the Left: "This is not the first time that I find myself the object of this vulgar expletive. As a Christian I am disposed to suppress the anger it arouses in me; as Chancellor, however, I resent such an unseemly interjection." *Pfui* is an expressive interjection, but for intensity, vigor and color we have better words. Interjections emphasize the audible affective tone and not the visible sign. They contain the maximum coincidence between phoneme and sound, that is, the sound label of the word is identical with its inner speech form and has a necessary character without being a symbol, the very opposite to proper nouns which hold on to impressions only by means of the sign without reference to empirical correlates.

As soon as Adam had relieved himself of his oath, he was startled by the crowing of the cock heralding the dawn. A ray of devotion darted into his soul, for the chthonic cock is the emblem of hope and reawakening. Although the most salacious and impudent of all the birds, he has been recommended to monks as an object of emulation, for he is an early riser, a busy scratcher, shuns night life and is mindful of his domestic obligations. The cock is also the national symbol of France and the universal emblem of deceived husbands. The cock's cry, which rent the air of that early Indian-summer morn, touched Adam's sympathy and he saluted the two-legged fowl and the power of his larynx and thanked the Lord, reciting the prayer: "Praised be Thou, God of the world, who gavest understanding to the cock to

distinguish the day and the night." It was in the second shrill cry
of the cockcrow (*cantium galli secundi*), however, that Adam
first felt the full penalty of his fallen state. For he could not identify the sounds of the cry confidently. The *cockadoodledoo*
which wafted toward his ear seemed to come from an alien
world which was not part of the flowing circle of reality. Was
the sound he heard a genuine feature of the world? Would it
still be there if there were no ear to hear it? Would it be differently interpreted by other hearers? Adam could compare
the sound of the cockcrow with the original, for the language of
Eden still tolled in his wounded ear. He had lost his innocence
but not his memory. And to his ear now the crow was not the
sound-picture of the original melody he had heard the day before,
but a clumsy, literary reconstruction which Chanticleer himself
would have regarded with amused contempt had he recognized
it. Of all the versions of that alarming matutinal noise, the English is the most fantastic, for the climate of England is said to
have affected the ear of its inhabitants. The initial explosive consonants are uttered with a cocksureness that is in keeping with
the nature of that ill-humored fowl, but the vowels are far-
fetched and the intonation faulty. The Fr. *coquerico*, Ital. *chic-
chirichi* or the Dan. *kykeliky* are equally fanciful, and the Algon.
pahpahahquau (I quote from memory) is a whimsical Indian
vagary. The cock's jubilant voice as reproduced by the oboe in
the second part of Haydn's *The Seasons* is generally regarded by
musicians as more worthy of the King of the Barnyard and
would, no doubt, excite a sympathetic chord in the most exacting
cock. I, however, cannot pronounce judgment on the finer shades
of this musical performance, since Nature has denied me powers
of discrimination in those marked gradations of harmony which
make us prefer one note to another—a bear, as the Russians say,
having stepped into my ear.

The relation between the sound of the cock's crow and its

conventional fixation in human speech, which puzzled Adam, was the subject of the philosophical dispute concerning the relation between sounds and the things they stand for, conducted in Greek under the banner of *phusei* versus *thesei*, in Latin as *natura* versus *consuetudo*, in German as *Natur* versus *Kur*, in Arabic as *ilhâm* versus *istilah*—a dispute later continued between the analogists and the anomalists, then between the nominalists and the realists, and today under the barbarous names of onomatopoeia, sound symbolism, clang-tint, phonetic congruence and the German designations of *Schallwortbildung* or *Lautsymbolik.* An unsuccessful attempt to introduce the new word *imson* (a telescoped form of *imitatio son*) has been made to describe the phenomenon, but on the whole the name *echo word* seems to be the simplest and the most descriptive. Those who hold to the "nature theory" insist that the sound of words are, in one form or another, imitations of reality and of the characteristics of an object. They therefore take interjections, expletives and imitative sounds to be the primary substance of human speech, as did Vico, who gave this theory its classical formulation, and the Romantics who followed him. Those who hold to the "convention theory" are inclined to emphasize the arbitrary and conventional nature of the linguistic sign (Saussure) and would supplant speech sounds with graphic algebraic substitutes (Hjelmslev). They point out that such instinctive emissions as interjections or imitative words form but a small part of our vocabulary and a dispensable part, and that such words are not necessarily primitive, for modern languages often show a greater disposition to create echo words than the ancient (*cuckoo* replaced OE *geac*). The problem is the subject of continued controversy, for it involves fundamental questions concerning the origin of language and the nature of man, questions which came to the fore immediately after the Fall when first man's ear was pierced by the crowing of the cock.

The First Oath and the Crowing of the Cock

When Adam came to himself after his expulsion, he found that he was no longer on speaking terms with Nature. This was brought home to him, as we have seen, by his involuntary itchings, his uncontrolled sneeze, his spontaneous oath and his faulty hearing of the cockcrow. The shock of the debacle had alienated his speech from the natural world. His words had lost their adhesive power and were running riot in the sentence. The noisy names were too big for his ear. Before him was the unending world of objects and within him the impenetrable subjective life of the spirit. His task now was to join these two incongruous realms by the power of abstract language, a complicated task, for the a priori did not gibe with the a posteriori. Only the day before, he had catalogued the inhabitants of the world and branded them with natural sounds, and today his hooded ear could not even decipher the cockcrow. And reflecting on the strange accidents of life Adam, enlisting the harmony of metrical language, broke into lament:

> O woods, O fountains, hillocks and bowers!
> With other echo late I taught your shades
> To answer and resound far other song.
> —"Paradise Lost," Bk. X

To be compelled to quote was a sign of Adam's mental embarrassment. He was ashamed of the paternity of his own thoughts, now that he no longer could rely on God's collaboration, and he masked his complaint with a quotation whose source he failed to acknowledge.

And yet Adam could not forget the sounds of Eden, his first home. For nothing is dearer to us than our own home and the sound of our own language. No greater calamity can befall a man than to be compelled to leave his home and learn an alien speech. And no man loved his homeland more than Adam and none suffered so much the pangs of exile. Even the hopelessly damned in the *Divine Comedy* were touched for a brief moment when they were permitted to hear the sweet accents of their Tuscan dialect. But Adam knew he would never again hear the melody of Eden and he bemoaned his speechless sentence as did Mowbray in *King Richard II,* banished and condemned to forego his native speech:

> And now my tongue's use is to me no more
> Than an unstringed viol or a harp;
> Or like a cunning instrument cas'd up,
> Or, being open, put into his hands
> That knows no touch to tune the harmony:
> Within my mouth you have engaol'd my tongue,
> Doubly portcullis'd with my teeth and lips;
> And dull, unfeeling, barren ignorance
> Is made my gaoler to attend on me. . . .
> What is thy sentence, then, but speechless death,
> Which robs my tongue from breathing native breath?

 # XIII *A Domestic Quarrel*

The truant pair now paused to look about them. Behind them was the flaming Garden, before them a rocky waste. Nature groaned and wept with them, except the moon, who callously laughed at the mundane tragedy below. For this God punished her by obscuring her light (which she henceforth had to borrow from the sun) and subjected her to an unending procession of waxes and wanes. This gives rise to the vexing theological problem concerning the cosmic consequences of human evil. Is Nature neutral in human affairs and indifferent or even hostile to man's fate? And how can this be reconciled with the love of God?

At any rate, the scene confronting the expelled couple was not conducive to good cheer. They were the original DP's, isolated, neurotic and impotent in the face of a cosmic conspiracy: the basic mood of man in all ages of upheaval. It is not surprising, then, that they fell into boisterous mutual objurgation, chiefly *tu quoque* (you're another!), outdone only by the shrieking of the hoarse-voiced birds above. It was fearful to listen to their hateful words. But why conceal this darker side of conjugal life? A domestic quarrel is a nightmare, and only the Devil can take delight in the bitterness it engenders. No cause is too trivial to be made the object of abuse, recrimination and endless pinpricks. Propinquity suffices to bring into the open our hankering after altercation. Women, who have a natural urge to propagate their own opinions, are not exempt from this imperfection in our nature. Nor does the sentiment of love banish pugnaciousness. It flourishes best in the warm atmosphere of family life where intimacy renders it more poignant and where the causes, though more trivial, are deep and malignant. It seems we were not made to live in peace with one another.

Eve was the first to speak. Hot drops overflowed her dark eyeballs as she spoke to her fellow traveler (in the old sense): "The serpent is to blame for our undoing. I ate what I should only have looked at. At first I would not give you of the fruit for I wanted to keep the knowledge of the gods for myself. But the thought of leaving you here to another Eve prompted me to seduce you so that we could face this world together. Better together in this wasteland than alone in lofty Eden."

To which Adam replied: "I have been betrayed by my Spare Rib, my curse-mate. Yesterday I was a person of eminence, today a wreck. But the Fall has not ruined us completely. We are deranged but not beyond repair. The Fall has made us eccentric but it has left us enough sense to enjoy the cooling touch of rain, the taste of cheese and the sound of the ticking of the old clock. In time the Lord will relent, for He needs us for His scheme of salvation. Our wisest course for the time being is to follow the advice laid down by R. L. Stevenson in his 'On the Enjoyment of Unpleasant Places' (having in mind parts of his native Scotland): 'When we are put down in some unsightly neighborhood, we must set ourselves to hunt out beautiful things with all the ardor and patience of a botanist after a rare plant. . . . We must learn to live with Nature as with a fretful or violent spouse; to dwell lovingly on what is good and shut our eyes against all that is bleak or inharmonious.' I should have taken a greater interest in flowers and grasses while still in Eden. But now there is no road back to the Garden; Eden is the uneaten apple."

To this Eve, who had by now acquired a taste for disputation, answered: "You have fallen into the passive error of overspeculation. Epistemology will never get you to ontology. General principles are not worth a damn. The world cannot be reconstructed by the power of conceptual thinking. Let us understand backward but live forward. You philosophize because you are tired and depressed. Why do we remain here in the shadow of Eden, between the glory and the dark? Since we have preferred science to ignorance, let us go forward. The first thing we must do is to form a club (not a social union but a cudgel made of hard wood) to defend ourselves against robbers. Then we must construct a language, which is the social counterpart of a club—to serve not only as a vehicle for your concepts but as a bearer of myths that will fortify our weakened instincts. Then we must lose no time in converting the dirt into gold, into a colorless, odorless, quantitative symbol that will make the whole world kin. You will make it and I shall spend it—this will satisfy your urge for conceptual abstraction and mine for practical achievement. This is our victory over the serpent. We shall plant another Eden in this barren waste." And inspired by the vision of a new Eden for her awaiting children, Eve broke forth in German lyrical verse, the language of those who are strangers in this world:

> "Magst du, Stern, versinken,
> Mag ich selbst vergehen!
> Meine Kinder werden
> Eden wiedersehen."

The two speakers being at the same time both the actors and the audience, the transgressors and the relators, it is difficult to form an impartial opinion on what had actually transpired. Not having anyone behind whose back they could talk constrained them to talk to each other exclusively—an intolerable strain on the firmest friendship. The presence of a third person would have altered the situation fundamentally by introducing an intruder who could throw his influence to one or the other and thus reap the benefit of discord (*tertius gaudens*). A third party (a gossip, a matchmaker or a Peeping Tom) would have destroyed the exclusiveness and secret solidarity of the original pair, and we would have been left a more detailed if not impartial record of the events of the day. Although we have no record of an eyewitness, we do have an account of an interview between Dante and Adam, a personal report made by the great poet himself when he toured Paradise some centuries later. Few interviews in history have been as significant from the standpoint of time, place, participants and the nature of the questions put. It is regrettable that the learned poet should have failed to question Adam concerning the particulars of his naming of the animals, the theme of this volume and our chief concern. Had I been found worthy of gaining access to that exclusive meeting, that would have been my first question. A record of first man's thoughts during the Animal Parade would have been one of the great monuments of literature and an important chapter in the mental development of primitive man. Even a plain, unvarnished account of Adam's thoughts during that brief half-hour would have been a welcome addition to the meager report in Genesis and a more powerful stimulus to the study of linguistics than Wittgenstein's *Tractatus*.

Dante hardly recognized Adam when his guide introduced him. Time had made considerable depredations in the Progenitor's appearance. He was architecturally dilapidated—he had hernia, fallen arches and an altered line of leverage, for his gait had shifted from his middle to his big toe. His nostrils sprouted whiskers and a solitary tooth in his upper mandible gave him a droll look. Furthermore, he was suffering from scurvy owing to a lack of vitamins, a deficiency which affected his body chemistry and created conditions favorable to hallucinations. Even if one does not believe in the Fall, it is apparent that man could not have been created in such a damaged state of disrepair. Part of the sour apple which had stuck in his throat and formed the largest cartilage of his larynx (Adam's apple) moved up and down as he recited long psalms. This vocal activity increased the amount of carbon dioxide in his lungs and compelled him to reinforce his flagging spirits with frequent draughts of what appeared to be a more potent beverage than Adam's ale, as a result of which his voice had sunk to a raw base. In this tone Adam broke forth into rhymed verse, the prophylactic against the miseries of life:

> Ale, man, ale's the stuff to drink
> For fellows whom it hurts to think.
> Look into the pewter pot
> To see the world as the world's not.

When the great poet was assured that he was speaking with Adam, "his Revered Sire," he put to him the following significant questions: (1) How many years have elapsed since that busy morning in Eden until the present meeting? (2) How long did the Garden delight the primal pair before they were evicted? (3) What language did the first couple speak? and (4) What was the precise nature of the sin for which they had been convicted? Adam, who had been listening to these questions through an ear trumpet, then revealed to his interrogator that he had spent 930 years on earth (a rare achievement for any man), 4,302 years in limbo on the borders of hell, making a total of 6,498 years since he had first been installed in Paradise; that the shadow of sin had eclipsed him in the noonday of his life, six or seven hours after he had been formed; that, having incurred divine wrath because of his desire to be like the gods, the gates of the sacred enclosure were shut behind him and his spouse at noon on the very day of his birth; and that the language they had spoken in Eden had been extinct many years "before the race of Nimrod began the unaccomplishable task," that is, before the confusion at Babel, where every man was stricken for his rebellion with an oblivion of his former tongue. This last statement contradicts the opinion which Dante had put forward in his *De vulgari eloquentia;* namely, that Hebrew was the original language of our Parents in Eden. This is the poet's only inconsistency in an otherwise sober piece of reporting. On the whole, the integrity and the unquestioned learning of the great Italian place his testimony beyond suspicion.

What language did the first pair speak in Eden? Every people has produced erudite advocates to prove that its language was spoken in the Garden. A learned Hungarian in the last century established to his own satisfaction that Hungarian was the language of Eden because the word in that language for scissors, *ollò*, looks like the very object it denotes. German, Swedish, Celtic, Danish and Basque scholars have all made the same claim for their respective tongues. A Belgian physician and scholar, whose real name was John Becan but who went under the pseudonym of Goropius, demonstrated that Dutch was spoken by Adam. His bizarre etymologies and fantastic linguistic theories gave rise to the verb *to goropize,* which became a synonym for fanciful derivations. Another method employed by scholars to determine man's first language was to note the first sounds uttered by an infant. Herodotus records that an Egyptian king had two infants placed in the care of a shepherd who was ordered not to speak to them nor permit them to hear human voices. The first word the infants uttered was *bekos,* Phrygian for *bread,* although to an impartial ear the sound is more like a child's imitation of a goat's bleating. It is difficult to believe that these infants, however precocious, would at that tender age ask for bread and not for milk, which is the normal diet of infants. The experiment was not scientifically controlled and hence is unacceptable. Moreover, its royal author had no right to snatch children for purposes of experimentation and expose them to such unnatural hardships. He should be rebuked rather than quoted. John Webb, an Englishman of the seventeenth century, employing more humane methods, demonstrated that Chinese was the first language of the race, since a newborn babe's first yell is (to the practised ear) the Chinese word *yä*. Goethe's poetical ear, however, heard this sound more accurately as *ää* (*Künstlers Erdwallen*). The testimony is conflicting. Those of us who are not scholars incline to the view that the first sound uttered by the male infant is *ä* and that of the female the long *e*, a distinction still characteristic of the sexes and corroborated by folklore wisdom:

> If it be a man, it says *a'a'*.
> That the first letter is of the name
> Of our forme-fader Adam.
> And if the child a woman be
> When it is born it says *e'e*.
> *E* is the first lettre and the hede
> Of the name of Eve that began our dede.

 XIV *Was Adam*
a Rationalist?

Adam was a rationalist in Eden. His reason, anchored in the solid
harbor of God's Mind, was invulnerable to the insurrection of the
flesh. His conquering cognition was not rooted to a particular
time or place nor governed by subjective considerations of sect
or party. He was born into the truth. He therefore had no need
of images or metaphors, except as a supplementary aid to inten-
sify or enhance the meaning of his words. The image was not
part of the word's meaning; the abstract was not derived from the
concrete image nor did the latter precede the former, temporally or logically, in the development of language. That Adam
saw the "red" sunset after he saw the "red" apple does not mean
that the color of the latter was transferred by him to the former
or that the first is prose and the second poetry. The color "red"
is an equipollent quality indigenous to both objects. We may
confidently assume that in Eden the abstract preceded the concrete. This can be seen from the German word *Abend*, which
means both *evening* and *west*, that is, both the time and the place
of the setting sun. Since the time of the setting sun can be conceived by itself without any reference to the place of its setting

but not vice versa, it is natural that the word *Abend* should first
be applied to the time when the sun's rays cease to illumine the
horizon and only subsequently to the area in which it sinks. Language was thus evolved on logical principles inherent in the human mind.

All this changed after the Fall. The mind's original connection
with God was broken and with it its rational frame. The Fall had
deranged the intellect and made it subject to the distractions and
irrelevant excitements of the sensible world. The thing-in-itself,
the dark kernel of being, was now inaccessible to the "meddling
intellect." An alarming shift had taken place in the intellectual
world, a shift from reason to imagination, from physics to bi-
ology, from propriety to sensibility—in short, a shift from the
outer to the inner man. Things had fallen apart and could not be
put together by reason. Adam could no longer confidently say
that the apple was round, sweet and red, but only that its form was
round, its taste sweet and its color red, the qualities of the apple
being held together only by the agglutinative power of the imagination which is summoned to help piece together our abortive
knowledge.

In order to understand the world Adam now had to turn his
eyes inward on himself and relate what he saw there to the ocean
of matter without, hoping through this introspective detour to
gain some assurance of reality. His starting point was his own
body. He began to speak of the mouth of the river, the brow
of the hill, the bosom of the sea and the eyelids of the dawn.
He transposed his head to the cabbage, his foot to the mountain,
his hands to the clock, his face to the world, his arms to the sea,
his bowels to the earth, his belly to flasks and fiddles, his neck to
bottles and woods, his ears to cups and walls and his tongue to
shoes, bells and flames; his nose, rump and spine to the prow, stern
and keel of a ship (Hung. *orr, far, gerinc*). His legs gave him
gambol, gambit and the *viola da gamba* (held between the legs,

Ital. *gamba,* leg plus *viol*), his toes *acrobatic* (Gr. *akróbatos,* walking on tiptoe). From his head he took *chapel, cattle, capitalist, precipice* (headlong), *mischief* (brought to a bad head) and *biceps* (Lat. *bi* plus *ceps,* two-headed, a muscle with two origins). The amazing versatility of the hand (Lat. *manus*), "man's external brain," furnished him with *manners* (a mode of *hand*ling), *emancipate* (transfer of ownership from one hand to another), *mastiff* (Lat. *mansuetus,* tame), a smooth-coated dog with drooping ears and pendulous lip, petted by the *hand; maneuver* (a *hand*iwork) and its shortened form *manure,* which is dung spread by *hand.* From his hands man also derived the digits, the dual number and the complicated system of decimals. The hand and its parts are no longer felt, but lie concealed, in the underlined words and parts of words of the following sentence: A well *thumb*ed, second*hand man*ual on *chiro*practics was *adroit*ly *palm*ed off on the *dextr*ous *surg*eon's *gawk*y, *sinister* but *hand*some *aman*uensis.

As man looked out on the natural world around him, his primitive imagination saw his head in *capes* (Lat. *capo, head*lands), his sides in *coasts* (Lat. *costa,* side), his bosom in gulf (Gr. *kólpos,* bosom; Ger. *Meerbusen*), his elbow in Ancona (Gr. *angkón,* elbow), his knee in Genoa (Lat. *genu,* knee), his mouth in Ports-*mouth,* his nose in Langen*ess,* his ear in Helsing*ör,* his eye in *En*geddi and his sleeve in *La Manche.* He saw the human contour in cosmography: England looked to him like an old shoe, Mexico a cornucopia, Long Island a fish, Cuba a stocking, Italy a boot, India an udder, the United States a wisdom tooth, Silesia like the palm of the left hand with the Riesengebirge for thumb; his innocent imagination pictured Europe as a virgin, Germany forming the body, Bohemia the navel, Denmark the thigh, Sweden the knee, Russia the skirt, Portugal the cap, Spain the face, France the bosom, England the left arm and Italy the right holding Sicily like a fan and chasing the fly Malta from the face of Sardinia.

Was Adam a Rationalist?

Primitive man's vocabulary, although imperfectly recorded, must have been replete with body analogies from *highbrow* to *heel*. When he had exhausted these, he reversed the metaphorical process and took back from Nature what he had lent her. Thus, he became aware of eardrums, windpipes, arteries, belly (OE *belig*, bellows), bowels (Lat. *botellus*, small sausage), the clavicle (Lat. *clavicula*, a small key that locks the chest), the jugular vein (Lat. *jugum*, yoke, which joins the body to the head), the uvula (diminutive of Lat. *uva*, grape), the thyroid (Gr. *thyreoeidés*, shield-shaped, the tonsils (Lat. *tonsillae*, shaped like stakes) and a frog in his throat (Fr. *un chat dans le gosier*). By this method man was able not only to establish physical analogies but to capture the things of the spirit as well. The highest flights of his fancy and his loftiest abstractions had their roots in the sensible impressions of the material things about him. Words had to borrow their wings from sense. In the breath of his body man found *inspiration*, in his eyes *vision*, in his eyebrow *supercilious-ness* and within him *courage* and *humor*. From the physical act of throwing he derived the abstract notions of *conjecture, subjective, abject* and *symbolic;* from the derisive gesture of wiping his nose he took the verb *to mock*.

Recalling some of the animal names from Eden, Adam extended them to apply to his fellow men: road hog, dark horse, guinea pig, lame duck, lounge lizard; to architecture: Fr. *oeil-de-boeuf*, an oval window; Ger. *Fledermausfenster*, a roof-window with wings; and other transferred uses, as: cat's-paw, white elephant, horseplay, pussyfoot, foxtrot. Even the louse has crept into his idiom in the sense of physical discomfort (*to feel lousy*) and in the sense of superabundance (*lousy with money*), referring to the prevalence rather than to the annoyance of that troublesome insect (Serb.–Croat. *stenica*, louse = nuisance). The Germans have treated the louse in a more radical fashion by making it a term of endearment (*Lausbub*), removing its sting by taking the pedicular parasite to their bosoms and killing it, so to speak, with kindness.

Man then left his body as the source of his analogies and sought his metaphorical fortunes wherever he could find them: he took *milliners* from Milan, *argosy* by metathesis from Ragusa, *currants* from Corinth, *tangerines* from Tangiers, *fustian* from *Fostat* near Cairo, *scallions* from Ascalon, *calico* from Calcutta, *bronze* from Brundisium in Italy, *poplin* from the papal town of Avignon, *cantaloupe* from the castle of Cantalupo near Rome where it was first grown, and *mayonnaise* from the town of Mahon in Minorca whence it has spread to all the world. These products have roamed far beyond the place of their origin, which is seldom remembered. Arcadia in the Peloponnesus has long since left its original precincts for an ideal state of rural felicity; Hesperides has found an abode in the West; Utopia (Gr. *ou*, no; *topos*, place), which is no place at all, has become a commonplace. A *hallmark* was at first an official mark stamped on gold and silver articles at Goldsmith's Hall in London to attest their purity, but now refers to any mark so used and figuratively to any evidence of genuineness or excellence. Billingsgate was originally the name of a gate in the vicinity of a London fishmarket, but was later transferred to the fishwives and their husbands and then to their abusive language and finally to any foul-mouthed person or violent abuse in general.

Man even conceived analogies in terms of family relations: the lion is the father of roaring, the echo is the daughter of the voice, the arrow is the son of the bow, vinegar is the son of wine, a smile is the daughter of a laugh. These genealogical metaphors, known in Arabic as *kunya*, are not uncommon in the Western languages: "soot, brother of flickering fire" (Aeschylus); "simony, the mother of whores" (Sotovagina); "coughing, stepmother of the chest" (Matthew of Vendôme); "I have said to corruption, Thou art my father: to the worm, Thou art my mother and my sister" (Job); "Safety will be the sturdy child of terror, and survival the twin-brother of annihilation" (Churchill); "Urine, the soft-flowing daughter of Fright" (Coleridge) and common proverbs, as: Necessity is the mother of invention, The wish is father to the thought, Money begets money, and so forth.

Verbal symbols rove far beyond their initial place of origin or denotation, and the strong early connection is often lost beyond recall. In the line from *Pinafore:* "Refrain, audacious tar, your suit from pressing"—we are not aware of the bridle in *refrain*, of the challenge heard and accepted in *audacious*, of the tarred canvas of the tarpaulin in *tar*, or of the pursuit in the ambiguous phrase *pressing a suit*. We have lost the common bond that once united *tulip* with *turban*, *pansy* with *pensive*, *one* with *atone*, *river* with *rival*, *mouse* with *muscle*, *two* with *twig*, *apricot* with *precocious*, *Attic* with *attic*. We no longer see the rhomboid in *lozenge*, the crane's foot in *pedigree*, the pebble in *scruple*, the furrow in *delirium*, the hard oak in *corroborate*, the star in *disaster*, the thunder in *astonish* and God in *giddy*. The image of the human eye is still visible in "the eye of the dawn" and in "the mind's eye" but has grown dim in "the eye of the needle" or in "the eye of the potato" and deprived of sight altogether in *daisy* (day's eye), *window* (wind's eye) and in the Ger. *Hühneraugen* (literally, hen's eyes), the corns or hornlike excrescences which plague Teutonic toes. A candidate (Lat. *candidatus*, clothed in white) is now as a rule dressed in black; a rubric (Lat. *ruber*, red) can be of any color; stirrups (OE *stīgrāp*, lifting ropes) need not be of rope; one can be nauseous (Gr. *naus*, ship) on land; we no longer drink at symposia (Gr. *syn* plus *pótes*, drink) nor sing ribald songs while lampooning (*lampoon* was originally a drinking song; from the exclamation OF *lampons*, let us drink).

A word can alter its original function and be put to uses for which it was never intended. The perfect tense of the Greek verb *eureka*, to discover, uttered by Archimedes on discovering the method determining the purity of gold, is now the official motto of California; the Latin verb *placebo*, I shall please, now refers to an ingratiating remark or to a medicine given with the sole purpose of pleasing; a *quidnunc* (Lat. what now!) is a gossip; a *quodlibetarian* (Lat. what you will) is now one who exercises his skill in disputation; *ignoramus* (Lat. we know not) has become a singular English noun; *quibble* (Lat. *quibus*, dative of *qui*, who) was a common word in Roman legal documents but is now associated with the quirks of the law; *recipe* (Lat. imperative of *recipere*, to receive) is found today only in cookbooks and at the head of prescriptions in its abbreviated form ℞; plaudit (Lat. *plaudere*, second person plural imperative, to applaud, *plaudite*, an appeal for applause made by Roman actors after a play) has been retained minus the final vowel as an expression of approval by clapping the hands. Even within the same language one part of speech may function for another. This is most common in the Fijian language where a noun can be used as an adjective (*kau* = wood, wooden; *tagane* = man, male); an adjective as an abstract noun (*dina* = true, truth); and particularly a verb as a noun (*vosa* = to speak, speech; *bula* = to live, life). In English one part of speech can be summoned to perform several functions with admirable economy and little confusion: *silver, iron, cotton* are nouns which assume functions as adjectives; *round* does the work of a noun, adjective, verb, adverb and preposition. A different function or meaning is indicated by a difference in pronunciation (*sewer, wound*), by shift of accent (*minute, invalid, entrance*) or by a change in the word order (*day off* is not an *off day; to see a thing through* is not *to see through a thing*) or context (the car stopped with a *jerk*, who got out).

Language, then, after the Fall could not be made to conform to logical principles, valid for all men. In Eden all things shone bright in geometric nakedness, a transparent world congenial to man's mind. In exile our muffled senses grope along the detours of metaphor and analogy in a vain effort to seize the essence of this loosely knit, hurly-burly world. Each language sees only a finite portion of the word's infinite variety, some hidden or neglected aspect, which reveals a personal bias or passing fashion but which is not grounded in universally valid, logical thought. If, for example, we take the word *apple,* whose origin is unknown, we note that in different languages the same fruit is seen in a different light. Phrases peculiar to English are: apple-cheeked, applerot, to upset the apple cart, apple-pie bed (a practical joke where bedsheets are so folded that one cannot get his legs down), to pommel (from apple-like knobs on hilts of swords occasionally used to administer thrashings: OF *pomel,* dimin. form of Lat. *pomum,* apple); Ger. *apfelförmig,* spheroidal; *apfelgrau,* dapplegray; *Apfelsäure,* malic acid; *Paradeisapfel,* tomato; *Sp.* manzana, apple, refers to a block of houses, *manzana de vaca* to an udder, and *sano como una manzana* means "sound as a nut"; Ital. *melo del duomo,* ball on the cathedral dome; Russ. There is not enough room for an apple = We're packed in like sardines; Dut. *een appelflauwte krijgen* = to fly off the handle, *voor een appel en een ei* = to get an egg for an apple, that is, for a song; Fr. *aux pommes!* = first rate, A-1; Lat. *malum,* meaning both *apple* and *misfortune,* lends itself to puns (Plautus *Amphitruo* ii.2: 89.91), and the proverb *ab ovo usque ad mala,* from egg to apple, corresponds to our "from soup to nuts"; Gr. *mélon* refers to cheeks, tears, tonsils, girl's breasts, swellings under the eyes and apple-shaped cups. Some forms are common to several languages: apple pie is in Norw. *eplepai;* Ger. *in einen saueren Apfel beissen,* to bite into a sour apple, that is, to swallow a bitter pill, is also found in Croatian and in Dutch; Adam's apple is in Norw. *adamseple,* and an apple of discord is in Dut. *twistappel.*

Even within the same language the meaning of a word depends upon some deep personal prejudice, a desired intention or vagary of the idiom spoken. Man's freedom to impose meanings on words is illustrated by the various definitions given to the vague concept *man:* Man has been defined as a political biped (Aristotle), a social contractor (Rousseau), an economic being (Manchester School), a trousered ape (C. S. Lewis), a talking animal (Carlyle), an animal with red cheeks so he can blush (Nietzsche) and a being which asks what being is (Heidegger). When *man* is used in a pregnant sense, without qualification, the definition is implicit within it, as: Let not the man in the critic be lost; Drudgery dwarfs the man; To find the man in men; He was a man, take him all in all. This is a man's world (*man* loses half of its meaning by excluding women); Men are grown-up boys (*man* loses its *raison d'être*); A mere man (depreciative pregnancy); Man is a noun (treated as a part of speech); Men are not men who . . . (the word forfeits its meaning and is given another *per nefas*); Man is only man when he is playing (diaphora); Hollow men or crawling men (oxymoron); Man or mouse (alliteration); She's not man enough to do it (catachresis). We hardly see the *man* in *man*ikin (diminutive of *man*, homunculus) and find it erroneously in *man*drake (whose forked root resembles a man and which is fabled to shriek when plucked). In gentle*man* or post*man man* has been reduced to a moribund, unaccented suffix. In wo*man* (OE *wif-man*, female man) it has acquired a spurious, undeserved significance as woe-man or womb-man.

The rationalist in language seeks to eradicate the accidental circumstances of race, nation, mood and private outlook and to achieve "a grandeur of generality" which would unite all men in one common fellowship based on our essential humanity. By purging words of their subjective emotions and intuitive images he would facilitate our insight into the truth. The sensible image is an adjunct and not an integral part of the word's meaning. Men are united by the free spark of reason that jumps from mind to mind and not by the parochial image produced by custom, tradition and heredity. Real knowledge does not lie in the sensuous affective features of a word but in its content elaborated by the soul. A word is to be valued, like a memento, not for its material or for its quaint design but for the associations it calls to mind: "My hands are of your colour; but I shame/ to wear a heart so white"— the primary meaning is not the color white but the moral quality of cowardice. For Romantics, however, this kind of generalized knowledge is of an inferior kind, "the kind idiots possess" (Blake). Truth lies in the bullion of the concrete image and not in the stamped abstraction. In Othello's soliloquy before suffocating his wife: "Put out the light, and then put out the light," the light on the wall is the sustaining focal point and the primary source of illumination, preceding temporally and logically the light in Desdemona's soul to which it is related as the incandescent tip of a match to its wooden body. A rationalist sees best without the seductive glare of the light on the wall: the stars are luminous at night. For the Romantics, on the other hand, the image is the bright center of the soul and the concept lies on the periphery.

In matters of language rationalists prefer comprehensive words which assemble the diverse aspects of an object and grasp them in their abstract totality, selecting a common trait as the unifying principle. For example, the typical English word *high: high thoughts* (grandes pensées), *high noon* (plein midi), *high wind* (grand vent), *high life* (la grande vie), *high respect* (respect profound), *to play high* (jouer gros jeu), *high-strung* (nerveux), *to live high* (vivre sur un grand pied), *high-minded* (magnanime), as well as: *high jump, highball, high Church, highbrow, high-toned, high latitude, high horse, highhanded, high and low, high and mighty,* and so on. Similarly, the French word *bon: les bons* (the righteous), *la bonne société* (well bred folk), *bon matelot* (able seaman), *le bon train* (the right train), *une bonne âme* (a simple soul), *à bon marché* (cheap), *trouver bon* (to find advisable), *c'est bon* (that'll do), *bon sens* (common sense), *bonne conscience* (clear conscience), and so on. Or, to mention only a few examples of the German *Haupt: Hauptbedeutung* (primary meaning), *Hauptbuch* (ledger), *Hauptfach* (major study), *Hauptfeldwebel* (top sergeant), *Hauptführer* (ringleader), *Hauptlandstrasse* (trunk road), *Hauptnenner* (common denominator), *Hauptprobe* (dress rehearsal), *Haupttreffer* (jackpot), *Hauptwort* (noun), *Hauptmann* (captain), and so on interminably. The English words *get, mind, put, make, do, keep* are such general words; *put up* alone has some fifteen different meanings. The Hebrew *kvd* (heavy) means *hard, burden, slow, liver, magnificent, multitude, dignity, gravity; dvr* (brisk) means *bee, speak, sanctum, desert, mouth, cause, pestilence, pasture, precept;* North Dakotan *xtaka* includes *to grip, to hold together, to kick, bind, bite, pound* and *be near.* Hebrew has different words for *taking off*, depending on whether one takes off clothes, phylacteries, hat, shoes, fruit from the tree, hair, veil, dust, ring, glasses or leg (amputation). English distinguishes various forms of locomotion: *gait, amble, trot, canter, saunter, meander, reel, shuffle, stagger, sway,* but some primitive languages have words to indicate whether the movement is made with swinging hands, shaking abdomen or buttocks, whether the walker is long-legged, hasty, corpulent or carrying a load. Romantics prefer the concrete word, one that reflects different desires, interests and points of view. The bricks of a chimney are not the same as those of a church nor the wood of the crucifix the same as that of a mast. The quality of oak in a heart of oak is not the same as in a head of oak. An ancient mariner is not an old sailor. Romantics would delight in the meticulous stercoraceous distinctions made by sportsmen when speaking of the various kinds of animal excrement: *buttons* or *crottels* (hare), *fiants* (badger, boar), *spraints* (otter), *snuttering* (apes), *bruzzing* (bears), *cigling* (locusts), *frantling* (peacocks), *clattering* (magpies), and so on.

Each language creates its own patterns through which it interprets the world and incorporates different aspects of existence in its grammar. English neglects differences of sex and social status but emphasizes mood and number; Nahuatl makes a distinction between animate and inanimate; in Dravidian the position of the speaker with respect to the object is an important element; in Semitic languages the action is regarded as repetitive, intensive or causative. Grammatical agreement is achieved in Greek by inflectional endings, in Swahili by a profusion of iterative particles and in Chinese by word order. Gothic, Russian and Turkish dispense with both articles; Hebrew and Greek with the indefinite article; Danish, Bulgarian and Armenian append the indefinite article to the noun. French has no superlative form, Yiddish no past definite tense, Hebrew no perfect tense and Chinese manages to get along without gender, number, tense or mood; Portuguese and Hebrew have no names for the days of the week and the Basque language has no word for *God*. Hebrew and Turkish do not distinguish between *Mrs.* and *Miss;* in Hungarian the titles *Mr.* and *Mrs.* are placed after the name; in English *lady* and *gentleman* can be used in the vocative only in the plural. Swedish has two words for yes (*ya, yo*) and so has the French (*si, oui*); English has two words for *yes* (*yes, yea*) and two for *no* (*no, nay*); Chinese has no word for either *yes* or *no*. Swedish and Spanish have two words for *but* (*men, utan; pero, sino*), German three (*aber, sondern, allein*). English insists on distinctions which other languages dispense with, such as: flesh —meat, sheep—mutton, small—little, much—many, last—latest, shadow—shade, tall—high, naked—nude, clock—watch, egoist— egotist, gender—sex, bunions—corns.

Disquiparancy, or heterogeneous correlates denoted by different names, is preferred by Romantics; equiparancy, or correlates with the same form, is a rational desideratum. Examples of the former are the separate names given to the younger sister or older brother (Siamese), to the different nieces and nephews (Dan.), to the paternal and maternal uncle (Lat. *patruus, avunculus*) and aunt (Lat. *amita, matertera*); the distinction between animate and inanimate (Sp. *pescado, pez,* live and dead fish), human and animal (Ger. *essen, fressen,* to eat; *sterben, krepieren,* to die), between male and female (Fr. *gendre,* son-in-law, *bru,* daughter-in-law), between singular and plural (Russ. *čelovek, ludi,* man, men; *goda, let,* year, years; Fr. *oeil, yeux,* eye, eyes), between past and present (Eng. *go, went; am, was*). Examples of equiparancy are: Fr. *chat, chatte,* tomcat, cat; Span. *muchacho, muchacha,* Heb. *yeled, yaldah,* boy, girl; Norw. *gas, gasse,* Croat. *guska, gusak,* goose, gander; Hung. *kutya, nöstény kutya,* dog, bitch; Span. *anda, andaba,* goes, went; Heb. *katal, kitel,* kill, murder; Span. *tío, tía,* uncle, aunt. Equiparant proper names are: Henry-Henrietta, Joseph-Josephina, Julius-Juliana; Adam-Eve are disequiparant but their first names Ish-Isha were equiparant. The rational principle in language seeks to avoid suppletion (the name given to disequiparant words which supply a deficiency) by various methods: by word position (Span. *pobre hombre, hombre pobre,* poor chap, poverty-stricken chap; Fr. *cher ami, livre cher,* dear friend, expensive book); by different stress (convíct, minúte, dígest), or by different pronunciation of the same word (wound, sewer, lead); by phonetic modulation (mouth—mouths, fall—fell); by context, where no external change is visible (the plural of *sheep;* the past, present and future tenses of *put* or *cut;* in an inflected language best illustrated by the Latin *malo malo malo malo,* I'd rather be in an apple-tree than a bad man in adversity).

Those who deplore this tendency in language toward uniformity and abstraction hold that a difference in outlook should find a difference in expression. This makes learning a new language a revolutionary experience. Human speech, being a reflection of national temperament, is the ideal expression of a people's character which can be discerned in the morphology and syntax of the language it speaks. Romantic studies, therefore, single out isolated linguistic forms for psychological speculation. Thus, the French word is taken to be a verbal diagram of the object it describes, the Italian word the gustatory expression of its taste, the English word a snapshot of the object in action, while the Spanish word conjures up the object itself. The volume of bulky words in the Greek language is taken as an indication of the encyclopedic mind of its speakers, the paucity of the Hebrew vocabulary the poverty of Hebrew thought. The imprecision of English is ascribed to the gray light and heavy mists of the country and reflects the spirit of accommodation which distinguishes its political life. Those who are sympathetic to the French language take it as the language par excellence, the verbal counterpart of the rationalistic cast of the French mind and its sense of proportion, corroborated in its use of the partitive which stresses the part as opposed to the whole (a peculiarity also found in Finnish). On the other hand, those who have conceived a dislike for the French profess to discern its exaggerated military spirit in its use of the future for the imperative. A partitive and a future imperative used in the same sentence (*Vous m'apporterez du café*) would clearly be an order given by an arrogant Frenchman imbued with both a rational and a military spirit. The great linguist Karl Vossler was fond of this method. One of his disciples, Leo Spitzer, used it to great advantage and obtained many illuminating insights, and the other, Eugen Lerch, was subjected to severe criticism for exaggerating unsympathetic traits in the French, in whose language he discovered infallible signs of fatalistic resignation (the impersonal use of *on*), proletarian tendencies (the use of the *il y a*), and so on.

This method of dissection has not spared the Germans. Their use of the past participle for the imperative (*Aufgestanden!*) indicates an even more deep-seated military spirit than is to be found in the French. Their inflectional system indicates the comprehensiveness of the German mind and their throaty sounds, which make heavy demands on the inner man, betray the depth and *Innigkeit* of the German soul. The German consonant shift, however, is the result of the inordinate drinking habits of the population. The German sentence, with its motley clauses and heaped-up verbs, reflects, in the opinion of those who have studied the matter from a psychological point of view (as Ernest Jones), an advanced stage of anal eroticism aggravated by a flatus complex. Spanish, on the other hand, is the language of realism. This is seen in its frequent use of the present participle (*estoy escribiendo*), its distinction between the copulatives *es* and *está*, between action and relation (*Fué llamado por su madre,* He is called by his mother; *Es amado de su madre,* He is loved by his mother; *Perdió a su hijo,* He ruined his son; *Perdió su hijo,* He lost his son), between the direct and the indirect (*Quiero á un criado,* I love a servant; *Quiero un criado,* I am looking for a servant). In general, Spanish character as seen in its language is distinguished by its restraint (the double accusative *Verle á Ud.*), its austerity (*No importa!* Never mind!) and its misoneism (*Sin novedad,* Nothing new). As for the Russians, their dislike for monotony is apparent in the roving accent which shifts lawlessly from syllable to syllable; their frugality is inferred because they have no verb *to have* and their hardihood from the absence in their language of the bourgeois words *business, respectability, week end* and *vain* (in the sense of *futile*).

In general, it is the Romantics who find fault with English. The theoretical basis for this dislike is to be found in the so-called "degeneration theory" according to which the more a language changes, the poorer it becomes. The adherents of this view deplore the breakdown in languages from the synthetic to the analytic, with the consequent loss of inflectional endings. Schopenhauer, who held this theory, thus took Sanskrit to be the purest and English the most degenerate of the languages of the world; and Adam Smith praised the eloquence, beauty and sweetness of the synthetic tongues. To its detractors English looks dry, bare and full of bones. To say that English has gained in vigor and simplicity by discarding superfluous forms (that is, by becoming aptotic), is like saying that an old man has gained vigor when his eyes have grown dim, his legs stiff and his ears deaf. The loss of inflectional endings is a forfeit of grandeur, the unsexing of nouns a capital deformity, the absence of ingratiating diminutives a symptom of heartlessness and the nebulous vowels of English a craven desire for compromise. English parts of speech have little or no personality and are hardly recognizable by their outward shape. English sounds conflict with the principles of human articulation and can be produced only with grimaces made by English mouths which have been constructed for this purpose (for example, *months, clothes, adscititious, phthiriasis*). Our language cannot be called musical unless the braying of an ass is considered musical. The sounds uttered by an Englishman spelling *rarer:* ah, eh, ah, ee, ah, are to a foreign ear indistinguishable from a jarring bray. In the matter of vocabulary we have become a nation of lowbrows, for we no longer recognize the roots of ordinary words as *asparagus, autopsy* or *orchid*, let alone *crepedarian, gry* or *gardyloo*. To meet this danger a group of English writers (including William Barnes, E. A. Freeman and the Bishop of Chichester among others) launched a literary movement, known as Anglosaxification, whose aim it is to avoid all words which bear the bar sinister on their escutcheon and to return to the unsullied speech of the country before the French conquerors (whom they find very *gall*ing) brought their language across the Channel:

> The cat came fiddling out of the barn
> With a bundle of bagpipes under his arm,
> Fiddle dee dee! Fiddle dee dee!
> The mouse has wedded the bumblebee.

The defenders of our tongue, generally rationalists, answer that if intelligibility is to be the criterion for admitting words into the language, then many *native* words would have to be excluded, as: *dingle, chipes, cooring* and *albeytarian*. It is of doubtful value to replace *oval* with *egg-shaped, library* with *book-hoard, conscience* with *in-wit, arithmetic* with *rimecraft* or *affability* with *hail-fellow-well-met-ishness*. The double-headed nature of English has given the language a Janus-like quality, "the elegance from Gaelic jade, the thews from Viking crew," apparent in its synonyms, one native and one borrowed: *blunder, error; fox, vulpine; fiery, igneous; childish, puerile; put off, postpone;* in its reduplicated phrases, half Latin half Anglo-Saxon: "in the Areopagy and dark tribunal of our hearts," "the circinations and spherical rounds of onions." Though the Norman invasion was a national calamity, it gave our language two keys of feeling. One who feels the language deeply can exploit this dual allegiance and move with ease from one level to the other:

> Therefore, you clown, abandon—which is in the vulgar leave,—the society,—which in the boorish is company—of this female,—which in the common is woman; which together is, abandon the society of this female, or, clown, thou perishest; or, to thy better understanding, diest.
> —*As You Like It,* V, i.

The drift in English to the uninflected, invariable word constitutes a linguistic advance. A sword is not a better instrument for being bejeweled nor a mourning band more meaningful for being embroidered. What English has lost in imagery and architectonic beauty it has gained in conciseness, economy and abstract vigor. In a conversation with Eckermann, Goethe remarked that the English talent for life was superior to the French talent for logic, and praised the English for daring to follow the bent of their own natures. Jenisch, in his excellent prize essay for the Prussian Academy in 1796, preferred English to his mother tongue, which he characterized as having a tendency to slip into unclarity, and Fénelon in his famous *Letter to the Académie* approved the English habit of borrowing foreign words. English is admired by those who hold that language should be an economical instrument for communication, unburdened by perplexing images. Rational writers who pride themselves on their solid judgment deprecate metaphor as an unfortunate legacy which prose inherited from poetry. Images weary the mind by making the commonplace appear passionate, and easily degenerate into literary conceits. Conservative authors, therefore, tend to avoid metaphors, especially mixed ones. Swift is said to have made the exaggerated boast that he had never used a metaphor in all his life. The French stylist Gautier was on one occasion moved to exclaim: "I am strong; I do not mix my metaphors." Careful critics take great pains to amend every mixed metaphor they find in the works of great authors on the theory that a tainted metaphor, like a virgin, should not show itself too familiarly. The attitude to metaphor influences the theory of translation. Goethe was of the opinion that the essential character of a translated work emerges in its perfection only when it abandons the literary trappings of rhyme, meter and metaphor and divorces the cognitive content from the esthetic form, the what from the how. He was therefore more pleased with Wieland's prose translation of Shakespeare, which shunned the metaphor, than with Schlegel's poetical rendering. Those who defend the mixed metaphor, on the other hand, feel no aversion to the promiscuous passage from one figure to another, as: to speak daggers, blind in the ears, the cheeks of his soul collapsed, the latrine of his soul, and so on. It is all an affair of literary prestidigitation, and success depends on insight and verbal skill. If the result is ludicrous or obscure, the fault lies not in the principle but with the author.

Naming-Day in Eden

In one of his short poems Pushkin relates how on peering one day through the cracks in the canvas of an old picture, which had been daubed over by the sleepy brush of some barbarian hand, he caught a glimpse of the hidden beauty of the original, and this recalled to the poet's mind the innocent days of his childhood before society had daubed him with its corrupt manners. The task of the poet is to peer through the surface elaborations of the palimpsest and discover the original image of the word, some hidden detail which would disclose its identity. To this end the poet reaches back to the distant cradle of human speech for the incandescent image which comes to him on the wings of metaphor. The luminous image unleashed is a powerful force in the lives of men. It reanimates dead words and stirs them to proclaim their origin with miraculous tongue. The metaphor on fire makes the dry bones live again. It restores Samson's shorn locks. It reminds fallen Adam of the springtime of the world when he gaily skipped among the green bushes of Eden, when all things spoke to him in natural accents. For a brief moment the songs of the birds that filled the air of Eden break forth once more, Nature's heart beats faster and God, Who had hidden Himself in a fog, comes forth and deigns to speak to man.

XV *Mumpsimus*
or Sumpsimus?

Dictionary digressions are a fertile source of information. While the eye is engaged in hunting down *galimatias*, a synonym for *amphigory* or *rigmarole*, it lights upon *galliambic*, which is defined as "a conic a minori tetrameter catatectic with anaclasis." Thus enlightened, the eye moves on to find that *opisthography* is "a writing on the back of a sheet of paper" and a fraction of an inch further that *opsimathy* refers to education acquired late in life. The roving eye is detained by *pretzel* which turns out to be the glazed cake that the monks in the sixteenth century gave to children (Lat. *pretiola*, reward) when they had learned their prayers, the twisted form of the cake representing the folded arms of the devout monks. As a rule, words deteriorate in time. *Fornication* has descended from the fornical architecture of the low-vaulted Roman brothels (Lat. *fornix*, arch) to the pudendous activity within. The most spectacular descent, however, has been made by *loft*, from the heavens (OE *loft*, sky) to the upper story. Few words rise in the development of language. The elevation of *urine* to *urn* from its humble place under the bed to its present respectable position on the mantelpiece, having lost its contents in the process and two vowels to boot, finds no warrant in any dictionary.

It was on one such lexical adventure that I by a sheer serendipity came upon the word *mumpsimus*. That erring reflection gave birth to this chapter, a mournful instance of the discrepancy often found between cause and effect. The word *mumpsimus* is derived from a story told about an illiterate priest who, on being corrected for reading *mumpsimus* in the Mass instead of the proper *sumpsimus* (first person plural perfect indicative of Lat. *sumo*), replied: "I will not change my old *mumpsimus* for your new *sumpsimus*," thus enriching the language with two whimsical words. The new word was put into currency by Henry VIII in the middle of the sixteenth century and in time acquired the meaning of an obstinate adherence to outmoded ways in the face of the clearest evidence that such ways are obsolete, hence unreasonably conservative. It gave us a much needed word to describe an unlovely trait in human nature which, because of the force of habit or the sin of pride, resents the intimation that the first impression we form stands in need of revision. It is regrettable that the word is no longer in common use.

The one-letter change in the priest's reading of the Mass is but one example of a host of such mutilations which have become part of the language, their imperfections hardly noticed and their origins completely forgotten. A formidable technical vocabulary has been created to catalogue these maimed forms: *prosthesis* prefixes an extra letter to a word (*squeeze* from OE *cwesan*); *aphaeresis* omits an initial letter (*squire from* OF *escuyer*); *paragoge* appends a letter (*against* from ME *ageines*); *apocopated* or *docked words* drop the last letter (*drear* from *dreary*); *epenthesis* inserts a letter in the middle of a word (*aghast* from *agast*); haplology omits medial letters (*barn* from OE *bere*, barley, plus *aern*, place). A historical mutilation which has become part of the language is the word *sneeze*, which was originally *fnese*, but

124

was misread after the initial *fn* became unfamiliar in the early fifteenth century and replaced with *neeze*, an *s* being affixed later to facilitate a greater expenditure of explosive breath and induce a sonorous swell. New words coined by erroneous division have come into the language, as: *nickname* for *ekename*, *apron* from *napron*, *adder* from *nadder*, *Nancy* from *Ann*. The final *s*, mistaken for a sign of the plural, has been dropped from some singular nouns: cherry (OE *ciris*, ME *cheris*), pea (ME *pease*), riddle (OE *raédels*, ME *redels*) and now Chinee for Chinese. An example from Hungarian is *csárda*, inn, from the older *csárdák* in which the final letter suggested the plural suffix. These are errors which have become part of the language. Most of the coined mutilations, however, never find their way into the speech of the people, for example, the numerous deliberate distortions of humorous writers who count on the forbearance of their readers, as: spoonerisms which maliciously transfer single sounds (to occupew the pie, kistomary to cuss the bride, a camel passing through the knee of an idol) or Winchellisms which add or lose a letter by telescoping two words (moneymooning, income-poop).

The priest's coinage throws a new apple of discord into the linguistic arena and raises a number of problems which will be touched upon in this chapter. Why did his new word gain favor and find its way into the dictionary when so many others have failed to gain acceptance? What part is played by the individual in the creation of language? Is language a social process removed from the realm of subjective whim? What are the criteria of correctness in matters of grammar and where does the final authority reside? Is language the product solely of an unconscious folk process inherited by the individual for his temporary use? Does human speech reflect the rational structure of the private world of the individual or is it a social institution built up by slow degrees for the sole purpose of communication? What right had the priest, as an individual, to tamper with language, a fortiori with the sacred text, and presume to recommend his error to the congregation? If the lapse was due to an involuntary seduction of sound or fraudulent association, how can we account for the priest's hostility on being corrected? What measures could be lawfully taken, and on what authority, to induce him to abandon his error and abjure his mumpsimus, at least while reading the Mass?

Adam's detractors in Chapter XI would be ready to point out that first man's errors were irremediable. He mistook the *walrus* for a horse (Dan. *hoalros*, horse), the rhinoceros for a Scythian ass, the caterpillar for a hairy cat (Lat. *catta pilosa*), the porcupine for a pig (Lat. *porcus*), the hyena for a hog (Gr. *hys*, hog), the owl for a feathered cat and the zebra for a striped ass. He had but a vague idea of gender (Eng. *man-o'-war* is feminine and Ger. *der Weisel*, the queen bee, is masculine). Then, for superstitious reasons, Adam refused to give the bear a proper name for fear of offending him, calling him Swed. *grandfather*, Esth. *broadfoot*, Finn. *honey-paw*. Man's unregulated imagination, resorting to analogy, called the camel *the ship of the desert*, the shark *the tiger of the ocean*, the parrot *the ape of the birds*, and the owl *the mother of Solomon*. These blunders, however, were not the result of obstinacy or petulance. They did not deviate from any codified grammatical norm or transgress social usage. Hence, we cannot speak of Adam's errors but only of his inadequacies which arose from the limits of his experience and the vagaries of his licentious imagination. The case of the priest is fundamentally different. He knowingly violated rigid rules laid down by the linguistic community and when called to account he did not defend his error on functional grounds of clarity, economy or expressiveness. He knew the hostility of the average man to linguistic innovations, that slight modulations of accent or some recurrent blunder of grammar are enough to ostracize a man socially and invalidate him from holding public office. Many persons, otherwise gifted, are rendered unfit for society because of defective articulation or the inability to distinguish between a cleft or uncloven infinitive. Incorrect usage is fraught with grave social consequences and a contempt for the rudiments of grammar is swiftly punished. As a clergyman he must have been aware of the dangers involved in an improper reading of Scripture, of the elaborate laws which regulate the writing and reading of the sacred text, of the millions of heretics who were damned for a diphthong. (The Hindus, mindful of the divine origin of their language, have a special prayer for the expiation of errors of speech.) He had no physical defect, so far as we know, which could have prevented him from pronouncing the fatal word properly. We must therefore assume that his disinclination to accept correction was rooted in willfulness. The priest may have had a desire to know the truth in the abstract but when confronted with a concrete manifestation which touched his person he flinched in its presence and proceeded to ignore and resent it. This is a common failing. Few mortals are thankful for being deprived of their cherished personal opinions, how much the less a priest, insulated as he is by an air of professional conviction.

What constitutes correct speech is the subject of controversy between the purists and impurists. Since the days of Protagoras of Abdera (one of the most original minds of the fifth century) who wrote a book on the correctness of names, the adherents of the purist doctrine insist that language, like morals or any other manifestation of man's moral nature, is subject to norms of reason and logic. A writer could achieve lucidity, urbanity, cadence and proper diction (the ultimate standards of the Augustan Age) by following the Aristotelian and Horatian canons which conform to the laws of good sense and human nature. This ideal is associated in English literature with the names of

Addison, Pope, Hobbes and particularly Dr. Johnson, whose literary labors were chiefly concerned with the effort to stabilize the language and clear it of its grammatical impurity, archaic vulgarisms and irregular combinations. In the preface to his monumental dictionary Johnson set forth the principle that in the determination of moot linguistic questions he would rely on the two invariable criteria of reason and nature as embodied in the works of the great writers of the golden age, those writers who flourished between the time of Sir Philip Sidney and the beginning of the deterioration of the English tongue which, as Dr. Johnson believed, set in at the beginning of the eighteenth century. For those who, like Johnson, take logic as their model the final test of correctness is reason as it manifests itself in good usage: the select usage of a certain period of history (Ciceronian Latin) or a geographical area (Parisian French) as it is incorporated in grammars, dictionaries and writers of authority. This is an arbitrary selection which the impurists find unacceptable. Writers of books and dictionaries do not create language or determine usage. They themselves, if they would be understood, must submit to its caprices, however monstrous. Reliance on rules and dictionaries is a comic habit of foreigners or a pathological vice of the learned. Linguistic disputes cannot be settled by an appeal to etymology because the original meaning of a word can be misleading (*Wer immer nach Gründen geht, geht zu grunde,* He who always goes to seeds, goes to seed). It is of doubtful advantage to the user of a language to know that *vegetarian* comes from a root which means *to thrive, radical* from *root* and *education* from *to lead out;* or that *hysteria* is related to *womb, matrimony* to *motherhood* or *poet* to *maker.* The literary practice of referring to roots is known as "the argument from conjugates," and Carlyle in English was a chief offender.

Language is too frail a reed to lean upon in vital matters. It is an imperfect tool created by ordinary men out of necessity in order to facilitate communication, and not by learned men to puzzle the mind with logical modes. Our living speech consists in a peculiar symbolic relationship which cannot be defined in terms of genesis or superimposed logical norms but must be sought in the actual operation of the linguistic mechanism at our disposal, subject to rules derived from custom, to follow which, however, is not a duty. From the impurist point of view our language is best when least tampered with by the learned and when its absurdities are left untouched. We shrink from speech that is too correct as we do from natures that are too chaste. A bit of negligence and disorder in our language, like a touch of lewdness in a woman, enhances its beauty. Sancho Panza, irked by Don Quixote's corrections, was moved to retort: "If you continue to carp at my speech and to find fault with it at every step, I'll not finish before the year is out. I have not been brought up at the court nor have I studied at Salamanca to know whether to add or subtract a letter from my words." The speech of uneducated men, imperfectly spoken, has often a charm and vigor unequaled by the refined speech of the learned, as for example the unadorned, honest speech in the moving funeral oration made by Parson Bullen over the body of Sut Lovingood: "We air met, my brething, to bury this ornery cuss. He had hosses and he run 'em; he had kiards, and he played 'em. Let us try to ricollect his virtues—ef he had any—an' forgit his vices—ef we can. For of sich air the kingdom of heaven."

The struggle between sumpsimus and mumpsimus may be viewed as the struggle between *language* as a social institution and *speech* as individual usage. Language as a historical institution tends to lose its cognitive content and to degenerate into a kind of verbal handshake. A French peasant, taking his last farewell of his deceased wife as she lay in the open coffin, was overheard saying to her, "Goodbye, dear, and take care of yourself." The comfortable rumble of a conventional commonplace had diverted his mind from reality, and although the meaning of the words was lost their hypnotic power remained. This verbal device is exploited in the Irish bull (a comminuted form of speech defined by a student howler as "a bull pregnant with humor") in which the words retain their plausibility despite the incongruity, as: The milestones should be placed closer together. This trend toward meaninglessness which impoverishes the language and threatens to destroy it as a means of communication comes about in various ways. A word can lose its meaning when, gaped at too long or admired excessively, it becomes conscious of its physical appearance and in its embarrassment loses its cognitive substance. A saintly word like *grace*, "consecrated by tears and cleansed by martyr-fires," can be put to shame by irreverent wits who, on being asked to say grace, merely repeat the word, thus depriving it of its operational value and reducing it to the status of an opaque sign. A word may also lose its meaning by having its specific content diluted, a favorite mode of definition among the Romantics: "Every book is a Bible, for every book is sacred; every man is a Royalist, for every man is fit to sit on a throne" (Novalis); "Every man is a priest insofar as he draws others to him" (Schleiermacher). Or a word is rendered meaningless by having its essence denied (civil service is neither civil nor service; the French horn is neither French nor a horn; Marx was no Marxist) or ignored (the Hebrew word for sonnet *shir zahav*, a song of gold, received its name only because the letters which form the word *zahav*, gold, accidentally add up to fourteen, the number of lines in a sonnet).

The confusions of sound due to mishearing play a large part in undermining the rational character of language. The general interplay of sounds whereby unfamiliar words are rendered meaningful by being melted into familiar ones, even though they may offend our etymological susceptibilities, is called Hobson-Jobson. This name is a mishearing of *Ja Hasan, Ja Hasan,* the cry of the Mohammedans in religious procession, as heard by the English ear, and although now only used in a technical sense, is itself a delightful example of many such words which have been assimilated to the English vocabulary. There are also: *pickaninny* for Sp. *pequeño niño; catsup* for Chin. *kwai-tchap; sparrowgrass* for *asparagus;* and humorous formations, as *fox pass* for *faux pas; Absolute and Abitofhell* for *Absalom and Ahitophel;* Russ. *voksal,* railway station, comes from the name of the London station Vauxhall; Hung. *viged,* vagabond, is from Ger. *wie geht's,* the greeting heard from German vendors in Hungary; Fr. *vasistas,* transom, is from the German question *Was ist das?* asked by a German foreigner in Paris pointing to a transom.

The irrational becomes most prominent in language when sense is sacrificed or subordinated to sound. Doubtful gnomic wisdom has been garnered by this method in proverbs where sound alone is the clue to the thought: Ger. *Träume sind Schäume,* Dreams are foam; Fr. *Poisson sans boisson est poison,* Wine goes with fish; Eng. *the masses are asses;* Rum. *soacra, poamă acră,* mother-in-law, bitter grapes; Hausa *zumu zuma ne,* a relation is as honey. An external phonetic resemblance can convert a senseless syllable into an independent word: *sue and pursue, cuss and discuss, texts and pretexts, sects and insects, wise and otherwise, the antics of semantics, every faction except satisfaction, any lock is better than wedlock, all his isms became wasms, to put the dent in accident, of all the hardships this was the hardest ship of all;* Fr. *sacre et massacre;* Ger. *Sucher und Versucher.* This humorous technique, which endows an inert limb with a life not its own, has a divine precedent in the creation of Eve from a lifeless rib. It is related of the great scientist Agassiz that, on being asked to identify a composite bug which had been put together by some undergraduate pranksters, he calmly replied: "Humbug!" In these examples the meaning is neither restored nor made transparent, but a spurious meaning is superimposed by an accident of sound. The bug of hum*bug* neither hums nor bites; it is no insect at all but a *bugbear* which, in turn, is neither bug nor bear but an imaginary goblin which excites a needless fear in children.

The influence of sound has made *male* and *female* equiparant (ME *masle* and *femelle*) and rendered acceptable such phrases as *to raise Cain* (cane) and *to eat humble pie* (umble pie is a real dish made of the umbels or edible parts of a deer). In France the columbine, *l'ancolie,* became the symbol of sadness, *mélancolie;* the poplar *le peuplier* owes its popularity to its similarity to *le peuple,* the people; and that the cock (Lat. *gallus*) has become the national emblem of the French since the Revolution is in no small measure due to the fact that it is a fortuitous homophone of Lat. *Gallus,* a Gaul. In ancient Rome it was believed that eating hare increased beauty (Lat. *lepus,* hare, *lepos* beauty) and in Greece the tree *ágnos,* which is phonetically similar to *hagnós,* chaste, was the symbol of purity. English has a number of veiled expressions which depend on phonetic analogy: I'm for Bedfordshire (to the land of Nod); He's born in Little Wittham (feeble-minded); He fetched a wife in Shrewsbury; He's gone to Hyde Park (hiding from his creditors); He's on the highway to Needham (on the road to poverty); He's gone to Ratisbon (died, rot his bone). The sound of a saint's name is often associated in the popular mind with the cure of some ailment or with some trade or profession: St. Expédit expedites affairs, *le patron des causes pressées;* St. Gallus is implored by those who suffer from bile (Swed. *gall* = bile), St. Augustinus by those who are troubled by an eye disease (Ger. *Auge,* eye), St. Lambert by the lame (Ger. *lahm,* lame), St. Ouen by the hard of hearing (Fr. *oüir,* to hear), St. Hâlin by the bandy-legged (Fr. *hâle,* bandy-legs), St. Cloud by those who limp (Lat. *claudicantem,* limping); St. Vincent is the patron saint of the wine growers

(Fr. *vin,* wine) and St. Michel the patron saint of the bakers (Fr. *miche,* loaf).

It now remains to note how conscientious writers have tried to restore or preserve a word's meaning in the face of the allurement of sound described above, or how speech asserts itself in its struggle with language. A word's meaning can be insulated from the taint of fraudulent associations by enclosing it in sanitary quotation marks or by affixing the adjective *true* or *real.* Both quotation marks and adjective may be omitted and the word itself repeated in its intensified or pregnant sense: What's what, Business is business, Keep politics out of politics, There are teachers and teachers, Coffee 10¢ but coffee, and the quaint perrisology eggs is eggs (a corruption of the logical formula $x = x$). The repeated word performs a kind of verbal leapfrog by leaping over the back of an empty word only to face about a moment later to restore to it its meaningful core:

What religion do I profess? None that you name.
And why none? Because of religion.

—SCHILLER

Treason doth never prosper! what's the reason?
For if it prosper, none dare call it treason.

—JOHN HARINGTON

Those who employ this figure of speech (epanodos) find it sounder to use an old established word like *religion* or *treason* with all its contaminating associations than to invent a new word or forego using it at all. Imperfect language is preferable to the terror of speechlessness.

The spurious accretions of a word can be sloughed off by appending cautionary phrases which restrict its range, as: so to speak, as it were, in the Biblical sense of the word, in the

Goethean sense, in the strict (highest, full, proper, widest) sense of the word. (Gladstone was once described as a good man in the worst sense of the word.) A word is said to be used in its Pickwickian sense when it refers to some esoteric or conveniently idiosyncratic meaning, as: "He is a miscreant in its Pickwickian sense of unbeliever" (Hood), thus removing the sting from an uncomplimentary remark. The Milesian sense of a word (from the indecent "Tales of Aristides of Miletus," the *Decameron* of antiquity) indicates an obscene or derogatory connotation, as: "the Queen is a topic, it were Milesian to say subject, whereon my loyalty shall never be lacking." Lenin's learned followers are fond of using words in their herostratic or counterrevolutionary sense, a historical allusion to Herostratus, a Greek incendiary who could find no better way of achieving fame than by burning down the Temple of Diana in 356 B.C. In the eyes of herostratists, notoriety is preferable to obscurity, and fame, though achieved on the gallows, is more desirable than oblivion. The burning of Joab's corn by Absalom, Harington's cloacal satire *Ajax* and the exploits of the hero of Sartre's *Le Mur* are herostratic feats.

Exegetes and existentialists resort to violent methods in order to confer meaning upon a word. The exegetes stuff a word with a significance not its own by extracting from it a meaning they had previously smuggled into it, in the manner of a conjurer who draws miles of threaded needles out of his mouth. This device permits theologians to expatiate on all subjects *in absentia* with an air of deep assurance and constitutes an essential part of hermeneutics pursued by exegetes with a zeal which excites our scorn today. This verbal legerdemain may be illustrated by the meaning attached to the empty Hebrew word *eth* (which serves merely as a sign before a definite accusative) in the verse "And God visited (*eth*) Sarah," to wit, that Sarah like this grammatical particle was still barren—an exegetical example of the dictum enunciated by Clement of Alexandria that the sacred books, like the blessed Virgin, are pregnant with hidden truths. The existentialists, on the other hand, do not impose an *alien* meaning on a word but attempt to restore a forgotten aspect or hidden secret by splitting a word wide open, using the hyphen as an ax: *re-sponsible, re-visions, re-search, gentle-man, at-one-ment;* Ger. *ent-sprechen, Fort-schritt, Schlag-wort.*

A less violent method of inflicting meaning on a word is through deliberate confusion or distortion. The figure of speech known as *chiasmus* inverts words: Stamp-collecting is the hobby of kings and the king of hobbies; Some co-eds pursue learning, others learn pursuing. A proverb, being a highly conventionalized, fixed formulation, lends itself to distortion. When applied to a far-fetched situation or dexterously turned to another purpose, it is known as a Wellerism or a Quoth Proverb, for example: "To err is human," said the housewife, as she shook ground pepper into the coffee; "Something is better than nothing," said the wolf when he swallowed the louse; "All's well that ends well," said the peacock when he looked at his tail; "*Virtus in medio,*" said the Devil as he seated himself between two old whores. Almost any proverb or set phrase can be thus perverted: Familiarity breeds children; Time wounds all heels; Flatulence is an ill-wind that blows good to nobody; She is every yard a queen; He is every other inch a gentleman; A straight line is the shortest distance between two joints; Many are called but few get the right number; Scratch a Russian and he'll appreciate the favor; Hitch your wagon to a movie star; The time is not out of joints; When is the younger generation coming to; and so on. Where the metaphor is still alive we have catachresis and the incongruity is apparent: Latin is Greek to me; My eye is my Achilles' heel; He made the grade while on the level; Those who are not up on a subject are usually down on it. Where the metaphor is moribund or dead the absurdity may escape detection: The old rake turned over a new leaf; She is superficial to the core. There is no end to the ingenuity that can be expended on this playful technique. A Beckett's *Comic History of England* is written entirely in this ludicrous vein as are the books of Julius Stettenheimer in German where this humorous technique is known as *Wippchen*.

Conscientious writers seek to preserve a word's distinctive meaning by the literary device of *disassociation*. We are accustomed to associating certain concepts arbitrarily: marriage with love, security with money, reward with merit, age with wisdom, belligerency with courage, children with innocence, the hero with the tenor role. To wean us from such misleading associations imposed by language thoughtful authors often employ disassociative phrases, as: aggressiveness with its pretense of independence, rudeness which is mistaken for wit, selfishness which fancies itself strong feeling; superiority without insolence; wellbred though learned—"He took the obscure for the profound, cruelty for strength, vagueness for infinity and the nonsensical for the transcendental" (Schiller); "Her heroism was exempt from temerity, her frugality from avarice, her friendship from partiality, her active temper from turbulency and a vain ambition" (Hume of Queen Elizabeth); and, on the tombstone of his dog Boatswain, who died of madness, Byron placed the following epitaph: "Near this spot are deposited the remains of one who possessed beauty without vanity, strength without insolence, courage without ferocity, and all the virtues of man without his vices." The antithetical, rhythmic balance of these disassociative phrases satisfies the harmonious movement natural to the literary mind, and this has probably been no small factor in endearing them to discriminating authors.

The sudden emergence of the concrete meaning of an abstract word serves to restore its original nonfigurative intention. This incongruous juxtaposition often produces a humorous effect, as Disraeli's ingenious retort on being warned by Gladstone that he will come to his end either upon the gallows or as the victim of a venereal disease: "I should say, Mr. Gladstone, that depends on whether I embrace your principles or your mistress." The opposite method of indicating the unexpected figurative meaning is seen in the phrase which describes Procrustes, the legendary Greek highwayman who tied his victims to an iron bed and then stretched or cut off their legs to adapt them to its length, as "a giant with a keen sense of the fitness of things." The figurative phrase "the key of one's heart" is taken literally in the following quatrain:

"You gave me the key to your heart, my love,
    Then why do you make me knock?"
"Oh, that was yesterday, saints above!
    And last night—I changed the lock!"

The two meanings of *face* are illustrated in Pascal's famous observation of a private idiosyncrasy which was fraught with historical significance, namely, that "if Cleopatra's nose had been shorter, the face of the world might have been different." The historian A Beckett records a practical joke, now happily lost in the mists of history, in which a facial metaphor was taken seriously, entailing alarming consequences on the perpetrator. The incident refers to a private matter into which it was thought that Sir John Coventry had no right "to poke his nose." His assailants thereupon maltreated the offender by severely pommeling his peccant nasal appendage, an extreme measure calculated to serve as a warning to those who take metaphors at their face value, as did the improvident young man in Arnold Bennett's limerick:

There was a young man from Montrose,
Who had pockets in none of his clothes;
    When asked by his lass
    Where he carried his brass,
He said: "Darling, I pay through the nose."

Entire plays and novels have been based on such puns. Gogol's short story "The Nose" rests on the coincidence of the literal and figurative meanings of the Russian idiom *ostavat'sya s nosom*, to go off with a nose, that is, to go off peeved or dejected. In Goncharov's *The Precipice* the lovers meet at a precipice, make precipitate decisions, run off precipitously, and so on. In more than forty plays Lope de Vega took proverbs as titles, illustrating in the development of the plot their deeper meanings and revealing in the denouement some unsuspected aspect, a method followed also by the great Russian dramatist of the last century, Ostrovski. This is a literary version of the *proverbes dramatiques*, popular in France in the latter half of the eighteenth century, in which the various meanings of a proverb are acted out in dramatic form and the participating audience led by degrees to guess the particular proverb on which the play depended. An ancient example of how the literal truth of a proverb is acted out is that of Polycrates who literally followed the advice of the Oracle of Delphi and "left no stone unturned" to find his treasure, and a modern illustration is to be found in James Laver's poem "A Stitch in Time, or Pride Prevents a Fall" in which the virtue of the heroine *literally* hangs on a thread.

The literal significance of a common phrase or proverb can also be evoked by placing it in an unexpected context, as Hamlet's "O that this too too solid flesh would melt" sometimes found on weighing scales, or Sp. *Yo te veo, bribón*, I see you, rascal, inscribed on many chamber pots in Spain. The literal phrase can also be brought to mind by an accompanying picture, as seen on the devices used in former times on the French coats-of-arms: *Je bless tous et nul me bless*, I cut everything but nothing cuts me (the literal meaning of the lemma being illustrated by the picture of a diamond); *Point par dehors*, Nothing outside (showing a pearl hidden within an oyster, as a symbol of modesty); *Agit dum agitur*, It drives and is driven (with the picture of a windmill). The modern cartoon, sometimes with the lemma omitted, is often a visual restoration of an idiom or proverb: a pot calling a kettle black, dark horses, lame ducks, monkey wrenches thrown in the works, politicians caught in bottlenecks, mending fences, keeping an ear to the ground, slicing baloney thin, and so on. In religious thought naked concepts are given a sensuous dress and an opaque intuitive form by the imagination in order to foster piety among the masses. To stimulate the religious imagination John Knoblauch of Strassburg, publisher of Luther's works, had as his printer's mark a verse from the Psalms: *Veritas de terra orta est*, Truth is sprung from the earth, with an accompanying picture of a naked woman issuing from a rock and pleading for help to indicate that Truth is the daughter of Time and does not come ready-made from Heaven.

The resistance of the priest's mumpsimus to society's sumpsimus is part of the larger debate between nature and convention, analogy and anomaly, nominalism and realism, purist and impurist, the normative and the functional, between the French School (Durkheim, De Saussure) and the Scandinavian School (Jespersen, Noreen). Those who are inclined to mumpsimus in outlook and basic temperament hold that the speech of the individual is primary and if adopted by the linguistic community it passes into language where it becomes the subject of historical grammar which is concerned with the life and evolution of words, their etymology and grammatical functions. In language the relation between a word and the object it designates is arbitrary, but in speech the relation between our idea of the word and our idea of the object is a necessary one. It is conceivable that Eve should have picked a cherry instead of an apple, but once having made a decision we are bound by her choice. Adam could have called the cock's crow by any other name, but having hit arbitrarily on *cockadoodledoo* the necessary reciprocal relation between the name and the sense constitutes for us the meaning of the word. It is not a question of actual fidelity (the crow of the cock may have had in reality a flutelike quality) but a relative fidelity which is not confined to sound-imitation alone. Sound is secondary and accidental to communication.

The antagonism between mumpsimus and sumpsimus is the linguistic counterpart of the deep division to be found in all areas of life and in all disciplines. It appears in ethics as hedonism versus asceticism, in politics as the freedom of the individual versus the authority of the State, in jurisprudence as natural law versus positive law, in literature as the validity of the soul's inner experience versus the chastening influences of social discipline. The ultimate question in this eternal struggle is who is to be the master, who is to sit in the saddle and who is to crack the whip—man or law, deed or logos, life or language, experience or expression, the rebellious priest or society?

# XVI *Janus Words*

"Woe unto them that call evil good, and good evil; that put darkness for light, and light for darkness; that put bitter for sweet, and sweet for bitter" (Isaiah 5:20). Then woe unto us all! For there are in every language many words couched beneath a double burden of two rival and simultaneous conceptions inimical to one another but endowed with equal cogency, words which conceal two faces under one hood. These Janus words are examples par excellence of the discrepancy between the syntactical and the logical categories and are regarded by skeptics as extreme forms of ambiguity, as examples of the incompetence of human speech to describe reality and as mournful revelations of the world of unreason precipitated by the Fall. In an effort to conceal this ambiguity and to make language more tractable to arbitrary manipulation, grammarians have imposed a logical blueprint on the multitudinous forms of living speech. But our language remains imperfect and full of deceptions, a fickle mistress unworthy of Logic's embrace.

One can run fast or stand fast; a fast color does not run at all; fast women are loose; loose is equivalent to unloose, bend to unbend, annul to disannul, ravel to unravel and shameful to shameless; to weather is to suffer wear or to resist wear; to be mistaken is to make a mistake or be the victim of one; to have a temper is to lose it; a fine needle is thin and a fine baby fat; in dusting furniture the dust is removed and in dusting a cake the powder is sprinkled in the form of dust; when we dress a chicken we either remove the feathers or adorn it with feathers, depending on the kind of chicken involved. All languages exhibit this peculiarity: Fr. *se marrer*, to be bored and to enjoy one's self; Ger. *sperren*, to open and to close; Gr. *skholé*, leisure and the work which is the result of leisure; Russ. *slovo*, word and secret; Heb. *bara*, to create and to destroy; Chin. *louan*, to govern well and to create a disturbance.

Much subtle logic and psychological ingenuity have been expended on this curious linguistic delinquency by many

An eminent Logician who can make it clear to you
That black is white—when looked at from the proper point of
view;
A marvellous philologist who'll undertake to show
That "yes" is but another and a neater form of "no"!
—W. S. Gilbert, "Utopia Limited"

Indeed, *no* often does mean *yes* (not only in the insincere assurances of after-dinner speakers: "I am *not* going to make a speech"), but: Sp. *cómo no* is an emphatic affirmative; Fr. *Il est plus malade que tu ne penses* or Swiss Ger. *Er ist kränker als du nicht denkst*, He is sicker than you (don't) think; and the Russ. *Bojus ne upali vy by*, I'm afraid you'll (not) fall—these render negatively what we express positively. In Sanskrit comparisons are expressed in the negative: firm not a rock = firm as a rock; not a dog = like a dog; that is, in the same breath that the comparison is made its justification in reality and the possibility of taking the comparison literally is obviated by an abrupt denial. This peculiarity can be used humorously: "School days, what memories do they *not* recall" (Benchley); "India, what mysteries does the name *not* suggest" (Leacock); "May I *never* be hanged, if 'twas *not* a comical sight" (Rabelais).

Linguistic polarity was known among the Greeks as *enantiosis*, or naming by opposites, whereby that which is to be understood affirmatively is stated negatively, and vice versa. The method of deriving words from their opposites was in vogue for many centuries and gave rise in Latin to many idle etymologies *lucus a non lucendo*, as *bellum*, war, is derived from *bellum*, beautiful, because it is the least beautiful, *quia minime bellum; caelum*, sky, comes from *celatum*, hidden, because the sky is exposed (or because it is hidden during the day?). The problem continues to be of some interest even in our day. Popular and extensive studies of the subject have been made in Egyptian by Carl Abel, who called the phenomenon *Gegensinn*, counter-sense. In Hebrew it is known as *l'shon hefech* and in Arabic, where it has been elaborated with great passion and detail, it goes under the name of *addad*. In English the subject has been noted, but not seriously studied, under the name of polarity, turncoat words, mirror words and oysterisms (referring to the hermaphrodite nature and erratic ways of the edible bivalve).

The problem of linguistic polarity, which at first sight appears as a mere verbal oddity, has been studied etymologically (how can one morphological type give rise to two logically contradictory meanings?), psychologically (how can two opposed concepts converge in one word?) and logically (how can *A* and non-*A* be identical?). The first method has provoked many venturesome etymologies; the second assumes the original existence of neutral words which contain within themselves two contradictory meanings as a magnet two poles; and the third method, employed by Carl Abel, assumes an underlying double significance for each word. According to his theory, primitive man was unable to conceive abstract ideas except by contrast, and hence was constrained to compose words in the manner of *oldyoung, bindloose, bittersweet,* indicating the part meant by a pertinent gesture or sharp vocal emphasis. Such an indication of opposites is a typical construction in the Mande language where a phrase is followed by its reverse: "My bird die not, he lives"; "You no good, you bad." This is similar to the interrogative English forms: "You're a Republican, are you *not?*"; "You're *not* a Democrat, are you?"

The theories put forward to explain polarity are blurred by excessive speculation. A number of ways, however, may be noted whereby words acquire two meanings, one the opposite of the other:

a. Linguistic erosion: in the general wear and tear of language words suffer severe mutilations, often losing entire syllables: Dan. *bil* from *automobil;* Hung. *költö* from *versköltö,* poet; Eng. *ink* from Lat. *encaustum,* purple ink used by Roman emperors to sign edicts. In phrases consisting of two words one word sometimes is lost: a *weekly newspaper* is called a *weekly;* Hung. *tokaji bór,* Tokay wine, becomes *tokaji* and *sertés állat,* pig animal, *sertés.* It is by such a linguistic accident that Fr. *pas, rien* and *personne* lost the *ne* which always accompanied them and thus converted to their opposites, so that now *pas un pas* means *not a step.* Similarly, Sp. *todavía* from *todavía no* has come to mean *not yet.*

b. Illicit associations: words with similar sounds are associated with one another in the popular mind. Thus, It. *pomi dei Mori,* apples of the Moors, became Fr. *pommes d'amour,* and was then translated to Ger. *Liebesäpfel,* love apples; Fr. *pipe de Kummer* (after the name of the manufacturer) became *pipe d'écume de mer,* whence meerschaum. In this manner *demean* was erroneously related to *mean, cutlet* to *cut, outrage* to *rage, wiseacre* to *wise, sultry* to *desultory, hiccough* to *cough.* Such associations are most deceptive when the antithetical meanings converge in one word, although derived from different roots, as: *to let = to permit* (OE *laetan*) and *to hinder* (OE *letian*); or *to cleave = to adhere* (OE *clifan*) and *to split* (OE *cleofan*).

c. Pure ignorance: words tend to stray from their original context and to lose the glue which attached them to definite objects. This is especially true of the so-called unmotivated English words as over against the motivated German words, as: *adultery, obituary, halitosis* versus *Ehebruch, Totentafel, Mundgeruch.* The English words are imageless and not explicitly formulated, hence concise, mobile and resourceful but also flat, bony and wayward. Thus, the word *phenomenal* originally referred to any observed event, hence *ordinary,* but is now used in the opposite sense of extraordinary. Similarly, *literally* is used by uneducated people in a metaphorical sense, resulting in a confusion which gave rise to the Irish bull about a priest "who was *literally* the father of his flock."

d. External, non-linguistic changes: a change in point of view due to changed circumstances may alter a word's meaning to its very opposite. A *siren* once referred to the alluring enticements of song, but is now the signal of destruction. In ancient Rome a *client* was a citizen who took orders from a patron; today he gives the orders. An *apothecary* (a pot he carries?), who was a general storekeeper in ancient Rome, is now returning to his former occupation in the modern drugstore. A three-letter man, *homo trium litterarum,* referred in the days of Plautus to a thief (Lat. *fur*) and now to an athlete at a university. In ancient Greece an *idiot* referred to a man who could *not* hold public office! It is interesting to follow the fortunes of the word *virtue,* which once denoted the manly qualities of courage and virility, but which, after the rise of Christianity, became a tame synonym for female chastity (a condition, it is rumored, that is maintained today only by divine intervention).

e. Irony: *A* speaks to B so as to convey one meaning to B and another to C. Thus, a good word like *precious* has become an intensive for something reprobate or worthless, as: *precious knave, precious little.* An ironical meaning is superimposed while the original significance is retained in the mind. This is difficult to detect in writing because we have no mark to indicate the ironical tone of voice. Hebrew, with its loose tenses, indeterminate vowel system and unwritten punctuation, delights in ironical ambiguity which by a change of punctuation converts a phrase into its opposite: "What we believe" becomes "What! We believe?" or "Private! No visitors allowed!" becomes "Private? No! Visitors allowed." This peculiarity of style is to be found also in the English metaphysical poets who may have been affected by their Hebrew studies.

f. Reciprocal transactions: English interchanges *rent* with *let, come* with *go;* Chinese and Hebrew *buy* with *sell;* Dut. *Kooper* refers to either buyer or seller. In German the prefix *er* may signify either the beginning or the end of a transaction: *erreichen,* to attain; *errichten,* to start building; *ent* or *em* indicates approach or separation: *empfangen,* to receive; *entkommen,* to escape. In Hebrew a slight change of the vowel in the intensive conjugation can change the meaning of a word to its opposite: thus, *to take root* becomes *to uproot, to sin* becomes *to expiate sin* and *to pitch tent* becomes *to strike tent;* a similar modification is found in Eng. *fall-fell* and in Ger. *Kopf-köpfen,* head-behead. Thus also Fr. *boucher* is *to mouth* and *to shut one's mouth;* Welsh *cefnu,* from *cefn,* back, *to turn one's back;* Gael. *durnim,* from *dorn,* fist, *to strike with the fist;* Eng. *to skin* is to remove the skin, and to *shell* peanuts to remove the shell.

g. Exaggeration: successive states of an action are often contradictory because excessive preoccupation with an object may include the removal of that object, so that a denominative verb could acquire a privative significance, implying the loss of the very thing denoted by the noun. Excessive labor expended on an object may turn it into its opposite: *quaint,* an abbreviated form of *acquaint*, at first meant *known*, then *cultivated, elaborate* and finally *odd* or *old-fashioned*, an imputation of eccentricity being given to that which is too skillfully wrought. There is a point at which studied workmanship or perfection goes over into its opposite, best illustrated by the ambiguous word *finish:* "God made man but Hitler will finish him"; "Sending his daughter to finishing-school finished the old man"; "A man needs finishing (circumcision) like a mustard seed needs sweetening or like wheat needs grinding (Talmud)." In these examples perfection is made equivalent to extinction or maiming, both senses being indigenous to the word *finish*. This can give rise to seemingly absurd oxymora: *a perfect ass, a finished misfortune*. The latter incongruity is illustrated in the following humorous story recounted by Freud: A suitor berates his marriage broker for having introduced him to a prospective bride who limps, for one of her legs is shorter than the other. The marriage broker, undaunted, brushes aside the objection with the following argument: "Let us suppose that you marry a girl with straight legs; what do you gain? You are in constant fear from day to day that she may fall, break a leg and be crippled for life. Consider the pain, the anxiety, the doctor's bills! But if you marry this girl, nothing can happen to her. You have a *finished* product." This device which converts a defect into a virtue may be called *alopecuria* (Gr. *alopekía*, fox-mange, baldness) after the foxes in the fable who considered the loss of their tails to be a mark of beauty.

h. Reciprocal relations of the senses and the emotions: the "love of God" can mean God's love for us or our love for Him; in "the untented woundings of a father's curse" the wounds may be the cause or the effect of Lear's curse. It is difficult to determine from Jonson's well known lines: "But might I of Jove's nectar sup,/ I would not change for thine" whether he would or would not change nectar for kisses. The senses intermingle: the olfactory with the gustatory (Ger. *schmecken*, to taste = Yidd.

to smell), the optical with the acoustical (Heb. *tsahal* = to shine, to cry; Aram. *nahar*, cry = Arab. *nahara*, daylight). Human emotions are notoriously ambiguous. We are influenced and used by the things we fight against. Thus, a bully often turns into a coward, intimidated by his own menacing gestures. The names Methodist, Quaker, Whig, Yankee, Tory and Contemptibles, originally epithets of contempt, were defiantly assumed and robbed of their sting. Those for whom the affront was meant repudiated the name by accepting it. In the history of religious warfare the dogmatists often borrowed their whole arsenal of argumentation from the heretics. For emotions are related to one another like the two drunks in Lincoln's story who managed during a scuffle to get into each other's coats. The ambivalent nature of the emotions, especially those of love and hate, has provided a fertile field for the psychoanalysts (the "lover's pinch, which hurts, and is desired").

i. Directions: OHG *rîsan* refers to a movement both up and down; Heb. *nigash* is to approach as well as to draw back; MHG *zogen*, to move, is related to *zögern*, to hesitate. In the Fijian language the same word is often used to indicate contrary actions, the difference being indicated by affixing directional adverbs, *mai* denoting direction toward the speaker, *yani* away from the speaker and *tani* some other place: *lako*, to go, *lako mai*, to come; *kauta*, to take, *kauta mai*, to bring, and so on. Height and depth are interchanged: Heb. *akev* is a heel and a footprint, *givah* a hill and a cup, for "nothing resembles a hollow so much as a swelling"; we speak of a *deep* sky and a *deep* well, the *height* of folly and the *depths* of despair; we are *highly* esteemed but *deeply* moved; *high* mathematics is *deep;* and *deep* thoughts are not the opposite of *high* but of *shallow* thoughts. The "downs" of England refer to the *high*lands (Gael. *dune*, hill). *Raise* and *raze*, *sustain* and *uphold* add *up* or boil *down* to the same thing. *Alto,* originally the highest male voice, is now the lowest female voice;

in Spanish *alto* is the traffic signal *to stop*, for traffic stops when
the policeman *raises* his hand. Among the ancient Greeks the
downward nod of the head signified *yes* and the upward nod *no*.
Does a fly creep *on* or *under* the ceiling? Should we laugh *up* or
down our sleeves?

Spatial concepts are commonly confused with temporal: Eng.
by and by formerly meant *nearby;* Fr. *maintenant,* now, *in the
holding of the hand.* Confusing the notions of time and space accounts for the humor in the following: She will wear her dress
no longer (time or length?); Don't cook the spaghetti *too long*
(not over three feet!); Stop swearing before my wife! (she should
be permitted to swear first); Parisian kills wife before mistress
(sticklers for protocol, the French!). A literary example of this
confusion is the word *after,* which is the comparative of *aft,* and
which first meant "more to the rear"; as: "Jill came tumbling
after." It then took on the meaning of behind, with the intent
to overtake, as: "After man came woman and she's been after
him since." It then acquired the meaning of "to overtake" in
the sense of "to take over," "to look after." The spatial meaning
was then transferred to the temporal, since that which precedes
us in space is behind us in time; that is, one who is *behind* us
arrives *later.* The future lies before us but comes after us. Hence,
*pre*historic belongs to the past, and our *fore*fathers are behind
us while our *descend*ants are before us, so that *we* should be called
the ancients, as Bacon pointed out, by a computation backward
from us. This may account for the confusion in the naming of the
generations (MHG *Enkel* is both grandfather and grandson; infants are often referred to in Yidd. as *grandfather* or *grandmother,*
zedele or *bubella*), a detail noted by psychoanalysis where the
subject is treated as "the fantasy of the reversal of the generations." The incongruity in the word *after* is exploited in the witticism about the preacher "who thirsted after righteousness"

(drank after the sermon) and about the sycophantic fox in the verse:

> When the cheese comes round
> You know it's after dinner;
> But (what is known to few)
> The fox is after dinner too.

Among the ancients Socrates attempted to restore to the word its unambiguous latent unity, to find the word within the word and establish its specific constant meaning. It was, however, characteristic of most of the ancients, especially Anaximander and Heraclitus, to dwell on the intrinsic ambiguity of language. Later, the Sophists exploited this duplicity for eristic purposes by first supporting one aspect of an ambiguity and then another by means of paradoxes. This literary mannerism generally flourishes in an age in which the objective view of life has broken down and the need is felt to justify the subjective criteria of judgment. Poets and artists also prefer the binocular vision of the universe implied in ambiguity because it enables them to bring to the surface some unexpected neglected aspect which would rouse us from our mental torpor, as the paradoxes of Nietzsche or Wilde. When such paradoxes are contracted into two words, generally an adjective plus a noun, we have an oxymoron: *wise ignorance, silent yell, perfect beast, inspired idiot, splendid vices,* and so on. The oxymoron has been found attractive by many authors: "O heavy lightness! serious vanity! . . . Feather of lead, bright smoke, cold fire, sick health!" (Shakespeare); "Dem Taumel weihe ich mich, dem schmerzlichen Genusz, Verliebtem Hasz, erquickendem Verdrusz" (Goethe). Among modern authors Chesterton is the one most addicted to this verbal manipulation: *loyal traitors, honest quacks, evil euphemisms,* and so on. The strength of this stylistic figure lies in the tension with which it compresses far-fetched ideas, in making *extremes meet* (itself an example as well as a definition of an oxymoron). It is a verbal gargoyle which smiles and frowns at once or, to change the figure, a thorny rose which turns on itself and inflicts a mortal wound. The Janus word is the paradox par excellence, the oxymoron compressed in one word, a one-word adynata.

The Janus word makes of human speech a slippery instrument. It is, however, the reflection of the double nature of man himself, of the contradiction that lies at the very heart of humanity. In Eden man knew no ambiguity. But when he fell, he became Janus-faced, a *parvus mundus* of opposites, perilously poised at the juncture of nature and spirit, the riddle of the crossroads, the glory and jest of the world.

XVII *The Pomological Scandal*

The terrible injury sustained by Adam in the Fall disrupted the harmonious relation established between him and God when they had first exchanged names. An incredible change had come over Adam. He had been thrown as out of a dice box into a framework of space and time, which was to be his new reference of orientation. God's call to him after he had sinned: "Adam, where art thou?" was not a divine request concerning man's ubication or geographical latitude, like that of the Isle of Man, but a summons to man to find his bearings in faith and to establish a center of coordination from which to enter into a frank, dialogic exchange with God. Adam remained silent because he was in no *position* to respond. This breakdown in communication was the first symptom of the secret enmity that now broke out between God and man, an enmity accompanied by a silent acrimony characteristic of theological disputes. Nothing less than man's soul was at stake, and every inch of the ground was disputed.

In this disagreement between the human and the divine many pious souls, conscious of the irreparable damage suffered in the

Fall, have found it expedient to abandon Adam and to throw themselves on God's mercy, for He is long-suffering and pities them that fear Him. We are unable to escape inherited pollution (having been in Adam's loins at the time of the embezzlement) and, what is more, disinclined to do so (being nailed down by our finitude). Not only have we no oil for our lamps but we have also lost the wick. We are not only penniless but in debt. But if we wait patiently and if possible cheerfully, God in His mercy will deign to stoop down to us (for we are too exhausted to rise to Him) and pierce the intervening opacity with the illumination of His grace. This is the dismal doctrine of Seminal Identity, and only a theologian can take delight in it. No wonder the prophets moan on their birthdays and curse the day on which they entered the world. (Tyrants are wont to celebrate their birthdays with some sinister act: Pharaoh on his birthday hanged the chief baker and Herod beheaded John the Baptist.)

All doctrines which deviate from this oppressive anthropology are tainted with the heresy of Pelagianism. According to Pelagius, a Welsh monk whose real name was Morgan, human infirmity is not an ingrained flaw inherited from fallen Adam but flows from a voluntary desire to follow in his steps. We sin *as* Adam did and not *because* he did. Adam's error is due to a regrettable inadvertency and the damage it caused is not beyond repair. The Fall weakened but did not dissolve the original collaboration between God and man. Since Pelagianism is concerned with palliating the turpitude of first man's transgression and removing the repulsive features from the doctrine of original sin, it insists that evil was prior to sin; namely, that the Devil, a fallen angel, had infected Eve with sin when she listened to him (the theory of inquinamentum), or that Adam had committed a number of light offenses preliminary to the fatal one (Duns Scotus), or that he had already had a preview of the Fall in his deep sleep during the Rib operation (Jakob Böhme), that far from being spotless and in perfect working-order in Eden, Adam was a sub-man, ancestor of the Neanderthal man (Irenaeus)—in short, God must have created an evil impulse in man which was functioning, albeit feebly, while he was still in Eden, else how could a totally innocent man be suddenly tempted to sin (and what a sin!).

Here we have the two eternal foci of the theological ellipse, representing the endless controversy between august God and feeble man. In this dramatic struggle between tormented man and his Implacable Antagonist many have conceded the victory to the latter from the very outset, for God is mightier than man and can trample him down: "Howl ye, for the day of Jehovah is nigh." There have always been those, however, who have stood by man with unfeigned allegiance and have dared to defy the Omnipotent. The words most often on the lips of the former are authority, destiny, sin, agony, guilt, the bitter taste of finitude and the infinite sweetness of obedience; the favorite words of the latter are tolerance, individualism, enlightenment, reason, the dignity of man and the indestructible richness of his native endowment. The heroes of the first group turn their backs on the world to follow God and obey His commands: Abraham who was ready to sacrifice his only son; Job who believed in Him though sorely tried. The heroes of the second group are those who gave their lives in the service of man: Antigone who invoked natural law; Prometheus who invented fire. Both sides agree that Adam's sin was grave and that the Fall well-nigh wrecked him. But their views are differently balanced. Those who are convinced that the human situation is radically evil believe that with the Fall Adam forfeited all the privileges attached to his unfallen state and hence has no claims on our gratitude. At the other theological extreme are those who hold that man is born with inclinations neither good nor evil but by dint of his God-given powers he is bound to rise higher and higher in the course of evolution. The central position between these two groups is occupied by the doctrine of *felix culpa,* according to which Adam's sin was more fruitful than his innocence (St. Ambrose). Our complicity in Adam's guilt is not denied but overcome—we are wounded yet saved, triumphant though fallen. More has been gained than lost in the drama of salvation: a second Adam has replaced the first; the virgin Mary has superseded the virgin Eve; the garden of Gethsemane has risen in the place of Eden, and the cursed tree has been supplanted by the blessed fruit, the cross.

These rival conceptions of the nature of the Fall have plunged theology into an essential disunity which reflects two extreme attitudes to human nature. On the one hand it is held that man's guilt lies in his alienation from God whose wrath he incurred through disobedience and that the evil in him is radical. On the other hand it is held that although the Fall dislocated Adam it did not extinguish the light in him which, if rightly used, will dispel the disconsolate gloom and lead him back to Eden. Rationalistic theories assume that evil will gradually be melted down by the progressive illumination of the intellect, for evil is a relative good and a prelude to virtue (Hegel), adheres to the sensible but not to the intelligible self (Kant) and is only an illusion of the finite mind (Spinoza). Every man, then, by taking thought can lay hold of eternity. This peculiarly optimistic modern view was not shared by the ancients who restricted the attainment of wisdom to relatively few men, the world being composed largely of fools. Romanticism places its faith in the uncorrupted instincts of man who is naturally good. Reason cannot redeem him from the unnatural corruption of society, for reason itself is corrupt. Men are united not by their alienable rationality but by their common senses through which they receive the facts that constitute the lifeblood of human knowledge. In the light of rationalism language, though it bears all the marks of poor workmanship, is an indispensable organ in the construction of reality and, if redesigned to fit logical principles, can serve as a basis for the rational understanding of the world, equally valid for all men. To Romantics, however, the language we speak is prior to abstract logic and the sounds of speech are associated with the concrete feelings and intuitions of historical experience. Romanticism transfers "the soul's metropolis" from the logos to the imagination which builds its poetic visions into the physical structure of the word.

But neither the theologians nor the philosophers accept Adam as he is, for they consider him corrupt or at best defective. The only ones who defend Adam are his fellow poets. They made music for their first-born brother as he lay on the thorny cliff, wretched, stunned, sunk in corruption and half crushed like a worm. They wrapped his absurd thoughts in engaging sounds and rhythmic dialogue. They persuaded him to accept this confused world of caprice and brute accident and make it worthy of his steel. They taught him metaphor to decipher the world and close the gap between spirit and nature. They celebrated man's *fallen* state in imaginative language. For though the Fall had wrecked the concept, it left the image intact. Better the frail world of the imagination than the insipid abstractions of Eden in whose shadowless brightness the tender plants of romance and poetry wither. Better to sing of the taste of the sour apple than an abstract disquisition on its pomological properties:

> And all was for an appil,
> An appil that he tok. . . .
> Blessed be the times
> That appil také was.

Our First Parents were now thrown upon their own resources. The miscellaneous facts which Adam had amassed earlier in the day while naming the animals were of little use to him now in his relations with Eve. Naming the animals was a cognitive function designed to secure dominion over them. Adam had labeled and catalogued the ox, formulated the general laws of its behavior and classified the typical traits of Oxhood. This knowledge is of immense value (to a bullfighter) but relentlessly pursued for itself it leads to materialism. It forces man to take his place in the Animal Parade, albeit at the head, where he could be reviewed en masse, then related with precision and objectivity to his fellow men on the basis of common, external characteristics, labeled with a noun and then relegated to a zoological category for politicians to manipulate. The inner man and his private judgments vanish as man is dissolved into his eccentric functions. All this is done to the accompaniment of a deadening terminology of science and economics, anxiously concerned with private and social felicity.

In contemplating Eve, Adam could form no universally valid rules of Womanhood to serve as a basis of prediction for future generations. For Eve could not be reduced to statistics. She had no stable nature. No man could plot her curve. Adam could only tell us of a particular Eve who confronted him at a given time and place, of *his* perplexities and *his* errors (which we are bound to repeat). Two oxen are always alike, two Eves never. The dumb participants in the Animal Parade spend their pedestrian lives now, as they did when they first marked time before our antediluvian Forefather, moving in the same reiterated linear progression. Eve's life took unpredictable turns and moved in spirals. The quadrupeds that passed before Adam early that morning were a spectacle to be viewed and reviewed, and then branded with sharp-edged nouns to reveal their common abstracted traits. She, however, was a vision to be recognized and admired with ever changing adjectives. Adam was not related to her as a merchant to his wares (she wore no price tag), as a host to his guest (she was here to stay), as master to slave (she was made to order but not to be ordered) or as a thug to his victim (they felt stirrings of love for each other). If the animals were the notes of a song, Eve was the melody.

The primal pair was bound together by the Word. When Eve presented herself, Adam did not transfix her with an arrowy name but extended his salutations and hastened to woo her with polite phrases and a low bow. He did not introduce himself to the ox nor inquire after the health of that caponized bovine. Indeed, he had spurned the horizontal brute the moment he named it. The ox had reacted to the sound of his voice, but Eve grasped the meaning of his words without losing a single phoneme and she answered him not with an involuntary growl or purr but in low tender notes of joy and hope. Adam's mind was now turned from thing-ward to Thou-ward. Had he imposed his moral nature on the brutes, he would have been an idle visionary; had he treated Eve as an abstraction and abandoned her to the natural sciences, he would have been absurd; and had he refrained from addressing her with the redeeming Word, he would have deserved our contempt.

By this time Adam knew where he stood. Eden, guarded by cherubim with flaming swords, was inaccessible to his foot and no kindly law could save him from the bitter fruits of his deed. He had been given the freedom to choose and he chose to disobey. That lapse cost him his prelapsarian bliss. The moral paradox of his situation was plain: he had been chased out of Eden because the exercise of his freedom proved fatal and he could not return to it because freedom is interwoven with evil and the inevitable consequences of freely chosen acts. Yet, all was not lost. Though guilty, he was still the Father of Mankind. He had not cracked under the curse nor expired at Eden's door. He still found enough strength to plant the cypress and the shittah tree in the stony waste, comforted by the vision of the Tree of Life which blooms forever in the heavenly Paradise. With his language he planted the standard of humanity amid chaos; with human speech he could record the growth of the dark seed to the luminous tree; with prayer he could pay homage to the Ineffable. He now knew that a tree had other uses than to bear apples, that all things have a second and finer harvest for the mind. Despite the terrors of his human lot, therefore, Adam remained adamant, even cheerful. He saw the jest in his former majesty and the glory of his present abject state. In time God would reveal Himself to penitent man, for their destinies are interlocked in the common work of redemption.

We cannot follow Adam in all his original and extravagant notions. But we can emulate him where he is least extraordinary, in his cheerfulness, penitence and humanity. This is the testimony he has left in our blood, and this the hidden resolution at work in our flawed but proud clay.